CUNNING

The *Blackadder* Programme Guide

By the same authors:

The Red Dwarf Programme Guide

CUNNING

The *Blackadder*
Programme Guide

Chris Howarth & Steve Lyons

First published in this form in 2000 by

Virgin Publishing Limited
Thames Wharf Studios
Rainville Road
London
W6 9HA

ISBN 0 7535 0447 2

A catalogue record for this book is available
from the British Library.

Typeset by Galleon Typesetting, Ipswich
Printed and bound in Great Britain by
Mackays of Chatham PLC

Contents

Acknowledgements

With thanks to John Molyneux and Martin Fairgrieve who helped out with reference material, not to mention everyone who made *Blackadder* – and the other series we've looked at in this book – in the first place. We've also trawled the Internet for handy bits of information, and would recommend a visit to Blackadder Hall at
www.blackadderhall.co.uk

Authors' Note

Blackadder has been a profound influence on both our lives. Before its inception we could often be found doing sponsored walks for charity, voluntary work at the local hospital or simply being milk monitors at Sunday School.

Then *Blackadder* appeared on our television screens, and it was a revelation. The series and its central character inspired a change of lifestyle: no more organising church jumble sales for us. We learned that, though being parsimonious and deceitful didn't always pay off, it was a lot more fun than being generous and kind. Now Virgin have given us the opportunity to compile the first ever reference book about Edmund Blackadder in his various incarnations and what more fitting tribute could we give to the talented creators of this classic comedy than to make some cash by sitting in front of the TV and taking notes.

Unfortunately, our cunning plan didn't quite work; we did have to put in a certain amount of effort, particularly when it came to tracking down those members of the Blackadder family – and there are many of them – who never appeared on the small screen. In fact, you wouldn't believe some of the sacrifices we made. Imagine the shame we endured when we had to buy tickets for the Millennium Dome.

Nevertheless, there remain several unanswered questions. For example, how does the Blackadder line continue when its members keep dying, apparently without having sired any children? We'll just have to assume that all kind of stuff takes place between episodes. In each era Blackadder is a very bad man who, without the threat of a historical version of the Child Support Agency, probably isn't concerned about having the odd illegitimate sprog here and there. More surprising is the fact that the Baldricks continue to thrive.

Some of you may also be wondering why, with their tradition of making versions of many of our best comedies (the sanitised *Men Behaving Badly*, for example), the Americans didn't buy up the rights to *Blackadder* too. Perhaps we should be thankful. Although the Americans excel at making comedies of their own (*Friends*, *Seinfeld*, *The Brady Bunch* etc), the only thing worse than an American adaptation of a British sitcom is a British adaptation of an American sitcom. As to the reason for a lack of a colonial cousin for *Blackadder*, we don't know that either. But since America hasn't really got that much history, the options would probably limited to a Pilgrim Father or a Wild West gunfighter.

Nor can we shed any light on the vexed question of what those superstitious actors are saying when the mention of *Macbeth* sends them into a frenzied routine in 'Sense and Senility'. But there comes a time when you just have to stop caring, and get the manuscript off to the publishers.

Chris Howarth and Steve Lyons

1: THE BLACKADDER FAMILY TREE

Roots of All Evil

In a time when you can sum up pretty much every new television series by saying which two older series it's a cross between, a show like *Blackadder* seems even more special. There had never been anything quite like it on TV before, and there hasn't been all that much like it since. A search for precedents, then, isn't going to reveal a long list of *Blackadder*-like comedies lurking in television's darkest past. Nevertheless, *Blackadder* probably wouldn't have existed, at least not in the form that we know and love it, were it not for the influence of certain earlier programmes.

The Progenitors

Other than an enduring ability to make people laugh, there isn't much to connect *Blackadder* with *Monty Python's Flying Circus*. However, it was a shared fondness for this anarchic seventies comedy show that brought together three students at Oxford in the mid-1970s. To satisfy a yen to perform and make people laugh, they followed in the footsteps of two of their *Python* idols, Michael Palin and Terry Jones, firstly by joining the Oxford Revue and then by setting off for the Edinburgh Festival Fringe.

Making up this trinity of novice performers were Rowan Atkinson, Richard Curtis and Howard Goodall.

Nowadays Atkinson, thanks partly to *Mr Bean* – a comedy that even Germans find funny – is an international star. We'll look at his post-*Blackadder* television career in Chapter Six.

Curtis is arguably Britain's top scriptwriter (Britain's other top scriptwriters might argue) who, when not busy scripting the most successful films in British cinema history (*Four Weddings and a Funeral*, *Bean*, *Notting Hill*), can usually be found organising Comic Relief or attempting to bring an end to Third World Debt. He also writes the popular TV comedy series *The Vicar of Dibley*, and in 1993 he received the prestigious Writers' Guild Award for best comedy writer.

Howard Goodall is an acclaimed and successful composer, with themes for comedies such as *Red Dwarf*, *The Vicar of Dibley* and *Mr Bean* under his belt. He can do dramatic themes, too. Remember Melvyn Bragg's *A Time to Dance*? No? Well, it was the one where Dervla Kirwan got her kit off. Oh, so now you remember it. Goodall also collaborated with Bragg on the musical *The Hired Man*, and you might have spotted him fronting some poncey music shows, probably on Channel 4; he's the one who looks like a young Rory Bremner.

It's perhaps no surprise, then, that the diverse talents of these three young men from Oxford were quickly recognised – but just think what they could have achieved had they gone to a great university like Hull.

A fine-tuned version of the Edinburgh show, *Beyond a Joke*, gained favourable reviews when it moved to the London stage in 1978. It would be nice, if a little scary, to imagine that the Curtis-scripted film *The Tall Guy*, in which Atkinson plays the sadistic comedian Ron Anderson, is an accurate depiction of those times. But fear of legal action means we have to say that it's only a movie – although Curtis has admitted that it is heavily based on his short-lived stage career as Atkinson's straight man, a role that he apparently hated.

With his unusually pliable face and mastery of funny voices, the versatile Rowan Atkinson was a cert for television. In 1979, his comedy prowess was spotlighted on ITV in *Rowan Atkinson Presents . . . Canned Laughter*, a one-off sketch show for ITV, but he decided against signing for a full series. Soon afterwards, he was offered the chance to appear in a new topical and satirical programme for the BBC, and this time he accepted. The show was *Not the Nine O'Clock News* – yet, although it too has come to be regarded as a classic, it also got off to something of a false start. By the time it became a series, Rowan Atkinson and Chris Langham's originally assigned team-mates Chris Emmett, Christopher Godwin, Willoughby Goddard, John Gorman and Jonathan Hyde had been replaced by Mel Smith and Pamela Stephenson. Langham left after one series and was himself replaced by Griff Rhys Jones for the rest of the run. The team in its final form is generally regarded as the definitive one, mainly because no one remembers the other lot being in it.

The show – an astute and often hilarious mixture of sketches, nice videos of equally nice songs and hedgehogs – was originally shown on BBC 2 opposite BBC 1's *Nine O'Clock News*. The scheduling was partly the reason for its title – that and the over-dubbed news footage and swipes at figures who might otherwise be appearing on the actual news.

Produced by John Lloyd and Sean Hardie, *Not the Nine O'Clock News* was an essential programme in an age when Mrs Thatcher was at the country's helm and when it was Ronald Reagan's fingers that were poised over the red button. Richard Curtis joined the show's talented writing team and, at Rowan Atkinson's suggestion, Howard Goodall was brought on board to provide some of the songs. The programme ran for four series, broadcast between 1979 and 1982, successfully hitting virtually all of its intended (and deserving) targets along the way. Although entirely different in its approach to comedy, it acquired a reputation as the funniest sketch show since *Monty Python*.

After *Not the Nine O'Clock News* ended, Pamela Stevenson got hitched to some hairy Scotsman. Mel and Griff, alias Smith and Jones, went on to forge a successful comedy partnership on TV starting with the series *Alas Smith and Jones*. Rowan Atkinson, Richard Curtis, Howard Goodall and eventually John Lloyd collaborated on a project of their own. Surprisingly, though, it wasn't to be another sketch show, but a sitcom.

A Fawlty Start

Nowadays, people are inclined to judge a comedy on its individual merits, whatever the idiom, but in the early eighties there was still a precious attitude towards specific types of humour – in particular a distinction between mainstream and alternative comedy – which resulted in demographically targeted TV comedy shows. Fortunately, *Fawlty Towers* – co-written by and starring former *Monty Python* star John Cleese – had shown that situation comedy was not the exclusive territory of mainstream writers, and in doing so had paved the way for the creators of *Blackadder*.

Set in a Torquay hotel (allegedly based on a real one in which the *Python* team had once stayed), *Fawlty Towers* is perhaps most notable for featuring a less than sympathetic protagonist in the shape of the hotel's owner, Basil Fawlty. The incompetent Fawlty is condescending and rude to everyone – apart from the rich or well-connected, to whom he is completely obsequious. Flouting the convention that viewers have to be able to identify with comedy characters, Fawlty became a television icon: only two series of *Fawlty Towers* were ever made (twelve episodes in all), but you wouldn't know it to judge by the number of times the series still pops up on telly.

No doubt the series was an encouragement to Richard Curtis and Rowan Atkinson: as they searched for the right idea in which to showcase Atkinson's acting talents, they concluded that his character didn't need to be entirely likeable. However, *Fawlty Towers* is far more important to us for what the creators of *Blackadder didn't* take from it.

After months of doing the logical thing and working on scripts with a contemporary setting, Curtis and Atkinson found themselves forever comparing their output to the efforts of John Cleese and Connie Booth. As Curtis put it, in a 1998 interview for *Radio Times*: 'After *Not the Nine O'Clock News*, we wanted to write a sitcom. The original idea was to set it in a detective agency. After writing for about a month we got so depressed by the fact that it was never going to be as good as *Fawlty Towers* that we decided to disguise that fact by setting it four hundred years earlier.'

And thus the course of history was changed. In more ways than one.

Historical Precedents

The BBC programme makers, apparently, weren't too keen on the idea of a historical comedy at first. They didn't think it would work.

Our first response to this revelation was to think of loads of British historical comedies that *have* worked – *Dad's Army, Hi-De-Hi!, It Ain't Half Hot Mum, Get Some In!* . . . er, OK, maybe not 'loads', but some – but then, they all have something in common. Set in the past they may be, but they were also set within living memory of their original viewers (even the obscure Barbara Windsor series *Wild, Wild Women* just about manages that). It's instructive to note that, when Jimmy Perry and David Croft's popular Second World War comedy *Dad's Army* first aired in 1968, it was closer to its period than the 1969-set *Hippies* is now. Arguably, then, the historical comedy as it existed pre-*Blackadder* owed much of its success to nostalgia (although that clearly wasn't thought the case for TV drama, which was allowed to swap time zones with impunity). By delving much further into the past, Curtis and Atkinson planned to lose that possibly vital element. Nowadays, it's unlikely that anyone would take such a risk.

Nevertheless, *Dad's Army* is often cited as a *Blackadder* influence. It is, inasmuch as it's always been a great influence on the work of Ben Elton. Elton, a self-confessed fan of the veteran comedy, would join the writing team of *Blackadder* for its second series (as we'll see in Chapter 3). Shades of *Dad's Army* would, of course, be most visible a few years later, when *Blackadder Goes Forth* boasted a First World War backdrop that could just about claim to reside in the living memory of some viewers.

In the meantime, however, the series that was now called *The Black Adder* found a home in the latter years of the fifteenth century, an era that even Cliff Richard would be hard-pressed to recall. Stylistically, it copied all those 50s/60s series with titles that began *The Adventures of . . .* (*Robin Hood, William Tell, Sir Lancelot*), with Howard Goodall being brought on board to provide a theme tune that deliberately harked back to such programmes.

Comedy precedents, though, are fewer and further between. The big screen offers a few – there are several historically minded entries in the *Carry On* series, and John Cleese and the *Monty Python* cast turn up again, transferring their brand of humour first to Arthurian and then to biblical times for the feature films *Monty Python and the Holy Grail* (1975) and *Monty Python's Life of Brian* (1979). On TV, we ought to mention the little-remembered *Carry On Laughing* TV series, which preempted *Blackadder* by featuring visits to the Court of Queen Elizabeth I and to the time of Cromwell and the Roundheads.

One series stands out, however, as the natural precursor to *Blackadder* . . .

Up Pompeii!

Beginning in 1969, the BBC 1 series *Up Pompeii!* was really a vehicle for the talents of the late Frankie Howerd. Its suggestive humour was very much in the vein of the classic *Carry On* films, which is not surprising as it was scripted by Talbot Rothwell, who wrote the best of them (on *Up Pompeii!* he was usually joined by his *Carry On Spying* co-writer, Sid Colin). Indeed, when Barbara Windsor guest starred in the episode 'Nymphia' – as the title character, obviously – it was easy to imagine that she'd just stepped off a *Carry On* set.

Rothwell had already successfully visited the Roman Empire in 1964's *Carry On Cleo*, so perhaps that's why the BBC was minded to let him do so again. Howerd played Lurcio, slave to Senator Ludicrus Sextus. Their relationship is similar to that between Edmund Blackadder and his master Prince George in *Blackadder the Third*, as a knowledgeable and canny servant is forced to help his powerful but foolish and largely ineffectual employer out of various scrapes, sometimes finding ways to benefit himself in the process. The setting is the Roman city of Pompeii in the first century BC (the actual year given varies, sometimes within a single episode; perhaps there was some disagreement at the time over exactly how long it would be until the birth of Jesus Christ!). One major difference between *Up Pompeii!* and *Blackadder* was that Lurcio didn't get involved with real-life historical figures and occurrences: indeed, he lived over one hundred years before the single event for which Pompeii is remembered, i.e., its destruction.

In any case, the series refused to be constrained by its setting. Although most incarnations of Blackadder would come to share Lurcio's distinctly modern outlook, they would never be half as obvious about it as he was. Unlike the other characters in his world, Lurcio was allowed to address the audience, react to them and even to be aware that they hailed from his future. For that matter, he even knew that his dialogue was scripted. This enabled *Up Pompeii!* to put Howerd's talent for stand-up comedy to the fore; he had a knack of making scripted lines look like humorous ad libs.

After two successful series, *Up Pompeii* (minus exclamation mark) was transferred to the big screen in 1971. Frankie Howerd starred, of course, and Sid Colin provided the script, but the part of Ludicrus was given to established film actor Michael Hordern, with Barbara Murray and Madeleine Smith taking over the roles of his screen wife and daughter, Ammonia and Erotica respectively. In a rare move that the *Blackadder* series would eventually emulate, Howerd recreated the Lurcio character as a modern-day figure, seen showing tourists around the Pompeian ruins at the end of the film. The original characters were also moved forward in time so that we could see Vesuvius going up after all, and killing the lot of them.

Two more spin-off films extended the 'reincarnation' theme to different time periods. In *Up the Chastity Belt* (1971), Howerd became a serf called Lurkalot during the Crusades, and, more familiarly still, his final incarnation took him to the First World War, in which he served as under-footman Lurk in *Up the Front* (1972).

1975 saw a one-off television special, *Further Up Pompeii!*, which reunited most of the original cast of the series (although Mark Dignam became the fourth person to play Ludicrus). A full sixteen years later, the rights to the format fell into the hands of London Weekend Television, who produced a second special – imaginatively called *Further Up Pompeii*, but note the lack of an exclamation mark again – that reunited none of the cast. Filmed shortly before Howerd's death, this episode was set during the reign of Caligula (AD 37–41, which makes it compatible with neither the series nor the film) and dispensed with all the familiar characters apart from Lurcio himself. As the script – by Paul Minett and Brian Leveson – has it, he has now become a freedman and is in charge of the Bacchus wine bar in Pompeii. He even has slaves of his own. However, far from being a fitting epilogue to a well-loved series, popular opinion has it that *Further Up Pompeii* is utter crap. And who are we to fly in the face of popular opinion?

Up Pompeii!

BBC 1, London Weekend Television (Second Special only);
1969–1970, 1975, 1991; 16 episodes;
35 minutes (Pilot and Season One),
30 minutes (Season Two), 45 minutes (Specials)

Lurcio (Frankie Howerd)
Ludicrus Sextus
(Max Adrian, Pilot and Season One;
Wallas Eaton, Season Two; Mark Dignam, first Special)
Ammonia (Elizabeth Larner, not second Special)
Nausius (Kerry Gardner, not second Special)
Erotica (Georgina Moon, not Specials;
Jennifer Lonsdale, first Special)
Senna (Jeanne Mockford, not Pilot or second Special)
Plautus (Walter Horsbrugh, Pilot;
William Rushton, Season One)

Written by Talbot Rothwell (not second Special),
Sid Colin (Seasons One and Two), Paul Minett and
Brian Leveson (second Special); directed by various;
produced by Michael Mills (Pilot), David Croft (Season One
and first Special), Sydney Lotterby (Season Two),
Paul Lewis (second Special).

PILOT EPISODE (1969)

Up Pompeii! (17/9)

SEASON ONE (1970; 7 EPISODES)

1. Vestal Virgins (30/3)
2. The Ides of March (6/4)
3. The Senator and the Asp (13/4)
4. Britaniccus (20/4)
5. The Actors (27/4)
6. Spartacus (4/5)
7. The Love Potion (11/5)

SEASON TWO (1970; 6 EPISODES)

1. The Legacy (14/9)
2. Roman Holiday (21/9)
3. James Bondus (28/9)
4. The Peace Treaty (12/10)
5. Nymphia (19/10)
6. Exodus (26/10)

SPECIAL (1975)

Further Up Pompeii! (31/3)

SPECIAL (1991)

Further Up Pompeii (14/12)

An *Up Pompeii* film was released in 1971. Variations on the character of Lurcio also appeared in *Up the Chastity Belt* (1971) and *Up the Front* (1972).

2: THE BLACK ADDER

With Many A Cunning Plan

In June 1999, archaeologists unearthed a banana skin apparently dating back to the mid-fifteenth century – a much earlier time than the tropical fruit was believed to have been eaten in this country. Many of the newspapers that covered the discovery chose to turn it into a *Blackadder*-related article (some pieces accompanied by anachronistic pictures of the wrong Blackadder, but that's the British press for you). Why they made this connection *en masse* isn't clear. Perhaps they imagined that the notorious slipping-on-a-banana-peel joke had been a comedy staple in those times too; either that or the writers weren't familiar with any real personalities from the period. What the stories clearly demonstrate, though, is *Blackadder*'s enduring popularity.

It is more than ten years since the BBC made the final series of the historical comedy. But like *Fawlty Towers*, *Dad's Army*, *Porridge* and a very select few others, *Blackadder*, in its various incarnations, has entered the public consciousness as an evergreen favourite that remains just as funny no matter how many repeat screenings it gets. At the end of 1999, readers of *TV Times* voted it their clear favourite in a poll designed to find the TV Show of the Millennium – and, significantly, it was *Blackadder* that was selected to appear as a big-screen feature in the prestigious, if controversial, Millennium Dome.

However, despite its current well-loved status and reputation, the viewing public didn't take to the series or its immoral protagonist straight away. The first six episodes – entitled *The Black Adder* – were not a raging success; in fact, the series faced immediate cancellation. But we're getting ahead of ourselves.

How It All Began

Having pressed on, regardless of all advice, with their historical comedy idea, Rowan Atkinson and Richard Curtis apparently had enough clout at the BBC to get approval for a pilot episode. Now, unscreened pilots for programmes that eventually get commissioned are only usually as interesting as the differences between them and the finished product. For example, the pilot episode of *Doctor Who* is mildly interesting because the Doctor wears a tie and is supposed to come from the 49th century – and, in the try-out for *Buffy the Vampire Slayer*, things are pretty much the same as in the series except that Buffy's best friend Willow is played by an overweight girl, so just a few pounds' worth of interest there. Anyway, you get the picture. And, whatever other claim it might have as regards being an important piece of history, the original episode of *The Black Adder* certainly fits our criterion to be very interesting indeed.

Produced by Geoff Posner, the thirty-minute episode was recorded in front of a studio audience in early 1982. Understandably, the production is entirely studio-bound; it even features an illustration of a castle to set the scene, which, apparently, is England four hundred years ago. The episode opens with Howard Goodall's now familiar theme tune, minus any vocals. The screen is filled with what appears to be a royal coat-of-arms dominated by a snake, until the camera pulls back to reveal that the image adorns the cover of a book. The volume is opened to display the legend 'The Black Adder'.

The storyline is essentially that of the second episode of the series proper, 'Born to be King' (pilot scripts are seldom wasted and invariably turn up in some form or other if a series is made), but set a century or so later. Information in the dialogue, regarding Prince Edmund's birth, dates the action to the middle of the sixteenth century. Even so, the identities of the English monarch and his consort are left undisclosed.

Although the cast list yields some surprises, Rowan

Atkinson, with a reasonably sensible haircut, is at the heart of things as Edmund, Duke of York. There are some similarities to his portrayal of the Black Adder of the original series, but in many ways the two are quite unalike. The Duke (he's never referred to as the Black Adder) is just as devious and has the same ambitions as his first-series counterpart, but you get the impression that left to his own devices he'd be capable of achieving them, if only the fates would desist from conspiring against him. Given that the greatest weapon of the Blackadder dynasty would prove to be their wit, it's strange to see this prototype version leaping on and off a table and wielding a sword like a low-budget Errol Flynn. To describe this persona as a combination of the first two official TV Blackadders would, admittedly, be simplistic, but not necessarily wide of the mark. As such, he actually comes across as a more plausible ancestor for the Blackadders to come than does the character as he was ultimately realised on screen.

The personality of Edmund's wannabe best friend Percy is already well defined at this early stage – which, when viewed in retrospect, makes Tim McInnerny's portrayal perhaps the most familiar aspect of the production. Apart from Atkinson himself and Alex Norton, who plays Douglas McAngus and would return to do likewise in 'Born to be King', the only other actor to graduate from pilot to series was Elspet Gray, who, as the Queen, is resplendent in Elizabethan finery. No, in fact she's resplendent in Elizabeth's finery; if it wasn't for the fact that a costume designer is credited, we might suspect that the pseudo-sixteenth-century setting of the episode was dictated more by the availability of costumes from the BBC's wardrobe department than by any other consideration.

If Percy is reassuringly familiar, then Baldrick is a total shock to the system. With Tony Robinson since having made the part so completely his own, it is impossible to think of anyone else filling his shoes. It is therefore unfair to make any critical judgements about Philip Fox's interpretation, particularly in an episode not intended for broadcast. It may only be due to Fox's casting, but Baldrick originally seems to have been envisaged more along the lines of a typical young squire.

Slightly more familiar is Edmund's brother, although he is known here as Henry and he comes across as slightly effete. As he has little to do in this episode, though, it's difficult to judge whether this is deliberate characterisation or not. Actor Robert Bathurst went on to star in the wonderful BBC 2 comedy series *Joking Apart*, and later made up part of the ensemble cast of Granada's comedy drama series *Cold Feet* (as David, the pompous one).

Rounding out the cast (no jokes, please), was policeman-turned-actor John Savident, who appears as the King. Considering his portrayal of *Coronation Street*'s Fred Elliot was not so long ago voted Best Comedy Performance at the inaugural Soap Awards, Savident plays the unidentified monarch surprisingly straight. Though, in fairness, his dialogue doesn't present a lot of opportunity to go over the top. In terms of scripting alone, it was his character who would undergo the most dramatic post-pilot revamp.

The pilot episode is an enjoyable, if understandably unrefined, piece of television. Only the slapstick play scene drags a bit, almost starting to look like a panto set piece conceived for Cannon and Ball. Anyway, someone upstairs at the BBC obviously saw the potential of *The Black Adder*, and gave the go-ahead for a six-episode series.

The rest, as we can't resist saying, is history.

Unnatural History

For the series itself, the action was moved back in time from the cod-Elizabethan era to 'the darkest part of the Dark Ages' in order to present a harsher environment. Most of the changes made for the costlier and more ambitious series were improvements. But – and of course this is said with the benefit of hindsight – had Atkinson retained more of the Duke of York's personality and mannerisms when playing the Duke of Edinburgh, he might have been more accessible to the viewing public. Perhaps *Fawlty Towers* had been an influence after all, generating the subconscious impetus to bung in a central character totally without appeal. While Atkinson is undeniably funny in the role, he doesn't generate much sympathy.

The events of *The Black Adder* take place between the years 1485 and 1498, but in the reign of the hitherto unknown, i.e. made up, Plantagenet monarch Richard IV. Edna, erm, Edmund, Duke of Edinburgh and Warden of the Privies, is the King's least favourite son, which out of two isn't that bad. The asinine prince, a man of no obvious ability, has ambitions of power and, in an attempt to boost his reputation, assumes an affected alias. Though aided by his equally incapable friend, Lord Percy, and the dung-gatherer-turned-squire, Baldrick, it will take one hell of a cunning plan for the Black Adder to achieve greatness.

Joining the series as producer, John Lloyd, another *Not the Nine O'Clock News* survivor, added a twist to the historical premise. Inspired by the Hitler Diaries – faked documents that had recently taken in a number of ostensibly intelligent people – he created their fifteenth-century equivalents. *The Black Adder*, he claimed, was based upon a recently unearthed document, which disclosed that the infamous tale of Richard III murdering the princes in the Tower was merely slander. Ironically, some historians are now questioning King Richard's reputation as a villain – so it's quite possible that the quite nice monarch as memorably depicted by special guest star Peter Cook in 'The Foretelling' might be closer than anyone intended to historical fact.

Lloyd's manuscript goes on to reveal that not only did one of the princes survive, but he grew up to become Duke of York, heir to the throne and then, after defeating the pretender Henry at Bosworth Field (traditional history has it that Henry won), King Richard IV. Apart from this single document – which would eventually turn out to form part of the more extensive Blackadder Chronicles – all other records detailing Richard IV's thirteen-year reign were destroyed by Henry VII when he finally did accede to the throne. Indeed, as Lloyd explained in *Radio Times* if not on screen, Henry ensured that those thirteen years were wiped out of history by putting the date back to 1485 when he reverted to the Gregorian calendar.

Unlike the pilot episode, and indeed most BBC comedies, *The Black Adder* had the advantage of a fairly substantial budget, some of which was provided thanks to a co-production deal with the Seven Network of Australia. Extensive location filming around Alnwick Castle on the Duke of Northumberland's estate accounted for a fair bit of the allocated money. As well as serving to enhance the reality of this 'situation tragedy', exterior shooting allowed the *Black Adder* team the freedom to produce their own takes on movies like *Witchfinder General* and *The Magnificent Seven*, which presumably wouldn't have been undertaken in the confines of a television studio.

Interviewed during the making of the series, Lloyd explained why *The Black Adder* wasn't going to be cosy family fare: 'People in the late fifteenth century lived with violent death as a matter of course. When a plague arrived up to a third of the population could be wiped out in a few months. This is a comedy dealing with matters of enormous seriousness.'

Co-writer Richard Curtis added, 'We want everybody to act it for real; we want it to be dramatic, exciting – and consequently absurd.'

And, in a rare interview, star and other co-writer Rowan Atkinson revealed: 'I love characters that are extreme and larger than life and very peculiar. But I like them to read consistently and real. You think this guy is a lunatic, but you are convinced you have seen him somewhere.'

Setting a precedent unique to the *Blackadder* franchise, the final episode of the first series concludes with the death of the eponymous would-be villain. Under normal circumstances, killing off a show's central character wouldn't necessarily be the best way to gain a second series. *The Black Adder*, however, was never your average programme, and ultimately this was to be the master stroke that enabled the lead to be periodically reinvented in subtly different personas – as we'll see.

Introducing the Cast

As noted above, the most significant cast change from the pilot was the recasting of Baldrick. As portrayed by actor

Tony Robinson, Baldrick would eventually rival Rowan Atkinson's eponymous character in the popularity stakes.

Appropriately enough for one of the stars of a historical comedy, Robinson's television career has been roughly split between comedy shows and history-based programmes. His interest in myth and legend was put to good use in his enthusiastic retellings of the life of Boudicca and the adventures of Ulysses for Children's BBC, and his love of the past helped to make the real-life endeavours of the trendiest and best-looking practitioners of archaeology compulsive viewing in *The Time Team*.

Robinson's versatility as a comedy performer came to the viewing public's attention in the groundbreaking Channel 4 sketch show *Who Dares Wins*. Following a one-off special in 1983 (featuring Brenda Blethyn and William Hootkins), this ran for three seasons between 1984 and 1986. While not as political as *Not the Nine O'Clock News*, *Who Dares Wins* was never afraid to get close to the edge. Like all the best sketch shows, its success owed a great deal to making a compatible team out of several talented individuals – the others being Rory McGrath, Julia Hills, Jimmy Mulville and Philip Pope. For a while, Robinson also had possibly the best job on television: he presented *Stay Tooned*.

Compared to his descendants, the Baldrick of the first series is a cerebral colossus. After playing the character for several years, Tony Robinson said, 'Baldrick has actually got stupider as the years have progressed. However, I know lots of people who have been through university who are as daft as Baldrick.'

Like Robinson, Tim McInnerny was destined to play more than one version of his character, the clottish Percy. Being a proper actor and everything, McInnerny has also appeared in lots of Shakespeare stuff, including the RSC production of *Twelfth Night* directed by Griff Rhys Jones and the film version of *Richard III*, presumably resisting the urge to play it for laughs. Other film credits include *Wetherby*, *Eric the Viking*, *One Hundred and One Dalmations*, *Rogue Trader*, and he played Max in *Notting Hill* (1999). His television credits include appearances in such classic series as *Edge of*

Darkness, *A Very British Coup* and Granada's *Sherlock Holmes*. He's also been in *Casualty*. Apart from *Blackadder*, his TV comedy appearances include a couple of *Comic Strip* episodes and *Tracy Takes On*. Having worn tights as Percy, it was no doubt easy for him to put on stockings and suspenders to play Frank in *The Rocky Horror Show*.

The newly created part of King Richard IV fitted Brian Blessed like a gauntlet – because there just aren't enough television roles big enough to make full use of the talents of the larger-than-life actor who is more likely to spend his weekend off climbing Mount Everest than doing the garden. Since playing PC Fancy Smith in the early episodes of *Z Cars*, Blessed has gone on to myriad film and television appearances both dramatic and comedic. Arguably, though, his most memorable roles have been as kings, warlords and the occasional emperor. He was King Mark of Cornwall in the fab kids' show *Arthur of the Britons*, Augustus in *I, Claudius*, Voltan, King of those flying blokes in *Flash Gordon* (1980), King Yrcanos in *Doctor Who* and the voice of the computer-generated Boss Nass in *Star Wars Episode I – The Phantom Menace* (1999). Fairly soon after *The Black Adder*, Blessed took on a role he was born to play: the eponymous pirate captain in *John Silver's Return to Treasure Island*, a television sequel to Stevenson's classic.

Blessed was granted equal star billing with Rowan Atkinson for *The Black Adder*. However, despite his spot-on casting and performance, there was never another *Blackadder* role quite like King Richard, so, sadly, he had no involvement with future versions of the series.

Playing the rather important role of Edmund's mother was Elspet Gray, and although ultimately *The Black Adder* didn't seem to owe much to *Fawlty Towers*, at least in Elspet it had one regular cast member who'd actually appeared in it. Gray's list of credits contains a few other comedy series, such as *Solo*, *Dinnerladies* and *Murder Most Horrid*, but she can more often be spotted in dramatic roles. You may remember her in *Poirot, Tenko* or *Inspector Morse*. We, of course, remember her as one of the Time Lords in *Doctor Who*. Like screen hubby Brian Blessed, she didn't return for future series of *Blackadder*; she did, however, have a part in Curtis's *Four Weddings and a Funeral* (1994). For *The Black Adder*, she adopted a foreign accent to play the Queen, who has overseas origins.

Completing the Royal Family was Robert East, who took over the role of (the slightly renamed) Prince Harry. East has worked extensively in the theatre, so it should come as no surprise that his CV lists an RSC production of *Richard III*. TV appearances include *'Allo 'Allo* and *Miss Marple* and, film-wise, he's been in, amongst other things, Joseph Losey's *Figures in a Landscape* (1970). Presumably the thankless role of Prince Harry didn't present much of a challenge to the actor. Of all the recurring characters that have appeared in *Blackadder*, the stolid, relatively humourless Harry is far and away the dullest. Edmund having a more popular older brother works in the context of the first series, but it's easy to see why a similar character doesn't appear in future *Blackadder* ensembles. The closest comparison is probably Lord Flashheart, who would occasionally turn up and be more handsome and popular than Blackadder, or indeed anyone else.

One other character features throughout *The Black Adder*, albeit uncredited: the Narrator, who serves to place each episode within its alleged historical context and whose rich tones are provided by Patrick Allen. In the concluding chapter of the series, Allen for once appears in the flesh, playing the Black Adder's arch-enemy, the Hawk. The Hawk seems like the kind of character who could play a significant role in *Blackadder* mythology, but there was to be no rematch in future generations (although the second series' Prince Ludwig has similar ambitions and possesses a comparable talent for disguise).

The Bottom Line

The Black Adder was originally broadcast on BBC 1 from June 1983. For their first transmission, the episodes 'The Queen of Spain's Beard' and 'Born to be King' were swapped around (presumably because the latter wasn't ready in time) and, as all six episodes are dated, shown out of chronological order. The correct sequence was restored for subsequent showings and for the video release, the latter displaying a very obvious renumbering of episode two.

While it didn't exactly break the boundaries of comedy, *The Black Adder* is quite a bold attempt to do something original and innovative with the sitcom format (not that it's a sitcom *per se*, more a historical comedy adventure). It certainly isn't the innuendo-packed gag-fest that the series would evolve into. Nevertheless, it provides a lot of laughs and has the advantage of a strong narrative thread that is lacking in future chapters of the Blackadder family history.

However, the series met with a mixed response from viewers, as letters to *Radio Times* indicated. Di Morris thought it 'superbly brilliant, side splitting, fabulous, hilarious and very, very funny.' But Mrs E Forbes wasn't amused. 'Utter rubbish,' she called it, and what's more, 'Rowan Atkinson's facial contortions made me feel physically sick.' Mrs P Greenwood didn't care too much for the series either, particularly 'The Archbishop', which she thought was, 'the utmost bad taste, offensive, blasphemous, sacrilegious – the lot.' However, the last word has to go to Lesley Wynne-Davis, who thought, '*The Black Adder* was the funniest thing since banana skins.'

In financial terms, *The Black Adder* was a prestigious show for the BBC, so naturally they hoped and expected that it would be a huge success. Well spent as the money was, though – even the squalor in *The Black Adder* has a look of quality about it – the ratings didn't live up to expectations. Consequently, there was no way the cash-conscious BBC could sanction pumping a similar amount of cash into a second series. For there to be any chance of a follow-up, the locations would have to remain unfilmed and William Shakespeare would have to be dropped from the writing team.

Because of its comparative failure, *The Black Adder* was all but ignored for a long time, almost as if those concerned wanted to forget it had ever happened. Eventually, after other *Blackadder* series had sold loads of tapes, the BBC relented and the series followed them on to video and then into a repeat slot, with the episodes in the proper order and everything. Now reappraised, the first series is embraced wholeheartedly as an important part of the *Blackadder* canon. Well, almost.

Guide Notes

For our in-depth guides to all the incarnations of *Blackadder*, we've looked not only at the exploits and histories of the characters involved but also at some of the recurring elements that have come to define the show: its cunning plans, for example, and the suspiciously modern nature of some of its supposedly historical humour. Surprisingly, given its superficial differences to the series that were to follow, we haven't had to rejig these categories at all to accommodate *The Black Adder*. The familiar trademarks are all pretty much there from the start, albeit sometimes in lesser quantities than we've become accustomed to: the series is a bit short on double entendres, for example, although there are cunning plans aplenty (it even says so in the lyrics to Howard Goodall's magnificent, strident mock action/adventure series theme tune). One aspect that would diminish with time is the evil nature of the show's protagonist; we've judged the wrongdoing of future Blackadders against that of their illustrious ancestor in a category called 'You Horrid Little Man', again inspired by the *Black Adder* theme (we considered calling it 'You Little Turd', after Richard III's opinion of Prince Edmund, but that would have been a bit harsh).

The Black Adder (Pilot)

Written by Richard Curtis and Rowan Atkinson;
produced by Geoff Posner.

Never broadcast.

Prince Edmund (Rowan Atkinson)
The King (John Savident)
The Queen (Elspet Gray)
Prince Henry (Robert Bathurst)
Percy (Tim McInnerny)
Baldrick (Philip Fox)
McAngus (Alex Norton)
Rudkin (Simon Gipps Kent)
Jesuit (Oengus Macnamara)

Four hundred years ago, give or take a decade: it's the
Queen's birthday, and her youngest son Edmund is organising a show in her honour. But it looks like it won't be all
right on the night – the Queen's favourites, the eunuchs, have
pulled out (odd as it sounds) and the Jumping Jesuits are the
best replacement Edmund can come up with. To add to his
trials, when the Scotsman Dougal McAngus returns from
killing foreigners, the King rewards him with Edmund's
Scottish lands. A new play is added to the entertainment: *The
Death of the Scotsman*, in which McAngus will play the title
role. Percy and Baldrick are assigned the task of bringing the
performance to a fatal conclusion no matter what. So, when
Edmund discovers that McAngus possesses information that
might be to his advantage, he has a tough time stopping his

henchmen from literally staging a killing. Armed with letters from the Queen to her former lover, Edmund believes he has proof that his older brother Henry is illegitimate. But his maths is slightly off and, to McAngus's surprise as much as his own, *he* is the bastard. An angry Edmund challenges McAngus to a duel – only to find himself in possession of a prop sword and at the Scotsman's mercy. McAngus agrees to spare Edmund in return for a grovelling apology. Later, a Frenchman is found to confess to forging the letters, so all's well again. Edmund shows his new friend McAngus what the inside of a cannon looks like.

Watch Out For (if you happen to get hold of a pirated copy, that is): Alex Norton, who plays the Scotsman Dougal McAngus in this episode and returns in the series proper to play the remarkably similar Scotsman Dougal McAngus.

Cunning Plans: Here we witness a defining moment in *Blackadder* history: the first ever cunning plan. The first two, actually. Appropriately enough, Baldrick gets the (cannon)ball rolling with the idea of getting rid of McAngus by showing him the inside of a cannon and then setting it off. Edmund's plan is more elaborate, given that it requires him to go to the effort of writing a short play, during which McAngus can be 'accidentally' murdered. And it doesn't even work. But Baldrick's plan does.

Cutting Comments: Calling McAngus a bearded Gallic warthog is about as abusive as this version of the Black Adder gets.

You Horrid Little Man: Edmund has no qualms about killing McAngus in order to have his lands restored, and so he does kill him. After inadvertently getting in the way of Edmund's machinations, Baldrick gets a kick in the groin and a chair smashed over his head while Percy finds himself dangling from a noose.

Double Entendres: With a noose about, naturally there are references to being well hung. Due to poor weather, the eunuchs have decided not to venture forth from Chester. 'No balls, that's their problem!' says Henry, stating what is obvious to everyone but himself.

Suspiciously Modern: The Jumping Jesuits' work of performance art could grace the stage of any venue at the Edinburgh Festival Fringe.

Prince Edmund: To be pedantic about it, he's never actually called the Black Adder. Although he does look the part, dressed from head to toe in black leather, Prince Edmund, Duke of York is never referred to by any other name. He isn't happy with his lot in life: if only his older brother Henry was a bastard, then he would be heir to the throne. Becoming King of England would be the ideal first step towards his ambition of ruling the world (and that's only half of it). Documentary evidence (which he burnt) suggests that he is in fact the illegitimate son of the Third Duke of Argyll. Having made such a good job of it the previous year, he is assigned the unwanted task of putting on a show for the Queen. His attitude to the artistes invited to appear at what is, after all, a Royal Command Performance is tough but fair: if they do it, they don't get paid; if they don't do it, they get beheaded. He has a reputation as a formidable swordsman and, when it comes down to it, he proves to be quite the swashbuckler – even if he does feel the need to fight dirty. Acting is not one of his strong points: when he appears on stage covered in a sheet, pretending to be a ghost, he isn't scary in the least.

Baldrick: Early signs of stupidity can be observed here. When Edmund sends him for a prop sword to use in his duel, Baldrick fails to realise that that is the one he should hand to Lord McAngus. His mistake almost costs Edmund his life, and almost gets Baldrick castrated. Baldrick joins Percy to take part in Edmund's play, taking on the role of Buttock.

Percy: He is prepared to assist in the killing of McAngus only because he fears the consequences of refusing Edmund. He nearly ends up getting hanged for his trouble anyway, when it all goes horribly wrong.

The King: After all the slaughter that has taken place, he is looking forward to the end of the war with the Spanish – because then he can start fighting the French. Oddly enough, not only does he request that his son's life be spared, he is aware of the fact that he is called Edmund.

The Queen: Despite her reputation for purity – it seems the King only got her to accede to sex by claiming it was a cure for diarrhoea – she has an adulterous past. She and her husband must still be close though, since his present to her (Shropshire) is just what she always wanted. A typical mother, she thinks Edmund is sweet.

Prince Henry: Born in 1526, Henry is obviously a cultured prince, who likes painting and enjoys a good dance.

Name Checks: That 'Gay dog of the Glens' Donald, Third Duke of Argyll must have been very tall because the Queen's letters refer to him as an 'enormous Scotsman'. Although Jerry Merryweather actually has four chickens in his act, Bernard the Bear-Baiter apparently lacks a bear.

The World According to the Black Adder: He particularly despises the Scots and their country. As for no longer being able to pass laws there, well, he wouldn't pass water over Scotland. Odd that, for someone whose father is Scottish.

Essential Knowledge: The Black Adder motto is given as 'Veni Vidi Castratavi Illegitimos', which roughly translates from the Latin as 'I came, I saw, I castrated the bastards'!

The Black Adder (Series)

Edmund, Duke of Edinburgh (Rowan Atkinson)
Richard, Duke of York/King Richard IV (Brian Blessed)
The Queen (Elspet Gray)
Harry, Prince of Wales (Robert East)
Percy, Duke of Northumberland (Tim McInnerny)
Baldrick (Tony Robinson)

Written by Richard Curtis and Rowan Atkinson;
directed by Martin Shardlow; produced by John Lloyd.

1: THE FORETELLING

First Broadcast: 15 June 1983.

Richard III (Peter Cook)
Henry VII (Peter Benson)
Painter (Philip Kendall)
Goneril (Kathleen St John)
Regan (Barbara Miller)
Cordelia (Gretchen Franklin)

1485: Edmund, Duke of Edinburgh oversleeps on the morning of the Battle of Bosworth Field. It's the first decent battle since he reached puberty so, accompanied by his new squire Baldrick, he sets off to catch the end. But the only person he kills is King Richard III, who was, of course, on his own side. As they hide the body, Edmund and Percy meet the vanquished Henry Tudor; without realising his identity, Percy agrees to help him for money. Edmund's father is crowned King Richard IV, unaware that his enemy lies wounded in his castle. Edmund, the new Prince, is surprised to find Henry in his bed, but at least the reward will be useful when he becomes 'The Black Vegetable' or something similar. In the meantime, he is haunted by Richard III's ghost, looking remarkably well for someone with a detachable head. At the evening banquet's ceremony of desecration, a portrait of Henry Tudor is brought forth, and Edmund realises who's been sleeping in his bed. By now, Henry has made his escape. Giving chase, the Black Adder encounters three witches who foretell that one day he will be King. Only after he's gone do they realise their mistake: they wanted Henry Tudor.

Watch Out For: Peter Cook is given special guest star billing as Richard III. A brilliant satirist, Cook, along with partner Dudley Moore, helped revolutionise television comedy in the sixties with the series *Not Only But Also*. Sadly, he died in 1995. Gretchen Franklin was only a couple of years away from acquiring her little Willy as *EastEnders*' Ethel Skinner – which was a similar role really, if you count Lou and Dot as the other members of the coven.

Cunning Plans: Sadly, the first real instalment of the Black Adder's exploits is completely devoid of cunning plans. There's the suspicion of a 'cunning trick' though, which will have to do. It involves Henry riding up to a castle flying Richard's banners, but it isn't particularly cunning anyway, as it gets spotted straight away. And in any case it turns out to be Richard flying his own colours, which isn't actually a trick at all. Wasn't worth mentioning really.

Cutting Comments: Well, Edmund calls Percy a 'brainless son of a prostitute', which we assume was meant as an insult and not simply a statement of fact.

You Horrid Little Man: 'A horse! A horse! My Kingdom for a horse!' quotes Richard III on Bosworth Field. Trouble is, the first horse he spots is Edmund's, and after that it's more a head that he's in urgent need of.

Suspiciously Modern: Battle averages are collected like cricket scores. Edmund is almost put down for a duck, before entering his hurried and dishonest claim to have killed four hundred and fifty peasants – who would unfortunately only count in the event of a tie. A pity then that Edmund didn't fight for the other side (as he'd earlier joked to the amusement of nobody) because killing the King would have surely merited a six.

Prince Edmund: In the morning he is merely the Duke of Edinburgh, but later he becomes a Prince of the Realm. He rounds off the day by getting an even sillier, but shorter, haircut and donning the black clothes that complete his transformation into the Black Adder. Although his lackeys Percy and Baldrick come up with ideas, the Black Adder claims the best ones as his own. Oblivious to his own shortcomings, Edmund considers himself the fastest brain, the boldest horseman and, despite the reputation of a certain earl from Norfolk, the bravest swordsman in the land. He believes that Richard III has singled him out for special greeting, when the King is in fact describing him as a 'little turd'. Even his own father plans to place him among the rabble as arrow fodder at the battle. Edmund is surprisingly brave about going into battle – until he arrives and sees people lying down instead of fighting, at which point he has a change of heart. Upon accidentally decapitating the King, he tries to reattach his head, to no avail. He doesn't cotton on to the witches' mistake at all, even when they call him a 'ruler of men' and a 'ravisher of women', but that's probably because one of them refers to him as a 'slayer of kings', which is spot on.

Baldrick: He meets Edmund for the first time. It is he who suggests 'Black Adder' as a more impressive alias for Edmund than his first idea (his descendants would surely have gone with the vegetable motif).

Percy: His prowess as a soldier is in doubt: at one point, he intends to use the severed head he's found to prove he has killed a nobleman at the battle. It is notable that Percy is more interested in obtaining Henry's cash than Edmund, who is more concerned with power.

The King: Richard, Duke of York is a staunch supporter of King Richard III, the uncle who used to bring him toys in a sack disguised as a hump. He has two sons, though he isn't really aware of the younger one, Edna. After the decapitation of his 'Uncle Dickie', he is crowned King Richard IV. Locked doors present no obstacle to the King: he's all man, albeit, according to the Queen, with very small private parts.

The Queen: She doesn't keep up with current affairs, otherwise she'd know that her husband's foe isn't called Henry Tulip. She is keen to meet Henry, and hopes to have a bath before his arrival; however, upon hearing that he'll probably brutally ravish her, she decides not to bother changing after all. It says much of her opinion of Edmund that she suspects him of having a sheep in his room.

Prince Harry: The Prince is quite a sentimental soul, as exemplified by his eulogy to Richard III, which refers to flights of angels and suchlike. He is afraid of spoons.

Name Checks: Having failed to earn any points at the battle, Edmund tries to take credit for despatching some unaccounted-for nobles. The list includes Roger de Runcie, Lord Thomas of Devon and Lord Yeovil. He also tries to claim responsibility for killing Warwick the Wild of Leicester, until Prince Harry mentions that he killed him, too. The Bishop of Bath and Wells – whom Edmund ill-advisedly claims to have maimed, before learning that he wasn't at the battle at all – gets his first mention here, and sounds less controversial than his Elizabethan successor. Edmund certainly didn't slay Lord Coverdale, who of course fought on the same side.

The World According to the Black Adder: He thinks like a winner; after all, the alternative is to be a loser, and to lose at Bosworth would, he expects, mean getting hacked to bits, his arm ending up in Essex, his torso in Norfolk and his genitalia up a tree in Rutland (a well-known destination for parts most private). He is determined to prove he is a man, but not, as Percy suggests, by letting people look up the Rutland tree.

Essential Knowledge: The three witches are listed in the credits as Regan, Goneril and Cordelia, presumably named after King Lear's daughters. Their prediction would prove accurate, albeit for all the wrong reasons.

2: BORN TO BE KING

First Broadcast: 6 July 1983 (originally shown out of sequence as the fourth episode).

McAngus, Duke of Argyll (Alex Norton)
Jumping Jew of Jerusalem (Angus Deayton)
Celia, Countess of Cheltenham (Joolia Cappleman)
Sir Dominic Prique of Stratford (Martin Clarke)
2nd Wooferoonie (Martin Soan)
3rd Wooferoonie (Malcolm Hardee)
Messenger (David Nunn)

1486: with the King away killing Turks, Edmund hopes to gain more power, but he only gets to boss around sheep (and even they don't take much notice). If that isn't bad enough, Harry orders him to organise the entertainment for St Leonard's Day. It's soon apparent that the turns will be less traditional than usual: the bearded lady has shaved and the eunuchs have cancelled. In their place, Edmund gets the Jumping Jews of Jerusalem, Jerry Merryweather and his four chickens and a play starring the Strolling Wooferoonies, *The Death of the Pharaoh!* Meanwhile, Harry rewards the visiting Dougal McAngus with some land for slaughtering a large number of Turks: Edmund's land, in fact. Naturally, McAngus must die. Having substituted real knives for stage ones, Edmund persuades the Scotsman to dress in Egyptian robes and take part in the play. But when McAngus mentions some saucy letters of his father's, which cast doubt on Harry's parentage, Edmund is forced to rush on stage with the fake knife and ad lib a less fatal denouement. He reads out the incriminating letters from Donald, Third Duke of Argyll to his mother even as the King returns. But there has been a minor miscalculation: it seems that it's his own parentage that is in doubt.

Watch Out For: *Have I Got News For You* presenter Angus Deayton, who later joined Rowan Atkinson in his stage show for a while. Deayton was once known as TV's Mr Sex – but not any more, which must be disheartening.

Cunning Plans: Baldrick and Blackadder vie with each other to see who can come up with the most cunning plan to get rid of McAngus. Baldrick's is cunningly simple: show him a cannon and blow his head off. Edmund feels that his own, which involves having the Scotsman portray Tutankhamun McPhearson in a revised version of the Egyptian play now titled *Death of a Scotsman*, is more elaborately entertaining.

Cutting Comments: Edmund reckons that McAngus is a 'carrot-faced, thistle-arsed Scottish orang-utan' and a 'thieving, stinking weasel'. Though for some reason he doesn't say it to the Supreme Commander of the King's forces' face.

You Horrid Little Man: When the eunuchs cancel, Edmund calls for an execution order, intending to have their remaining bodily extremities removed. Brandishing a knife, he offers to show Percy what his insides look like, which is partly Percy's own fault because he does admit to being curious about their appearance. Later, Edmund makes a proper attempt to stab his friend, but picks up a prop knife by mistake. He also intends to stab McAngus in the bladder; in order to pursue him, he shoves his mother off her horse. He eventually takes up Baldrick's cunning cannon-based plan.

Double Entendres: When the Queen talks of 'the great brown ox, steaming and smouldering all night long,' she doesn't mean the meat course at the feast.

Suspiciously Modern: The Jumping Jews, as in the pilot.

Prince Edmund: He was born in 1461. Not only has he subsequently become Duke of Edinburgh, but he's also Laird of Roxburgh, Selkirk and Peebles – until Harry hands Roxburgh, Selkirk and Peebles over to Dougal McAngus. Edmund shouldn't be too upset though, for it seems that he'll be keeping it in the family: all the evidence points to McAngus being his long-lost half-brother. It is clear that he's taking the whole Black Adder role seriously, as his tunic has a snake entwined around a sword embroidered on to the sleeve. He has never learned Greek. One of his prized possessions is an autographed picture of Judas Iscariot, and he keeps a caged dwarf in his room.

Baldrick: He may originally hail from Chigwell. He drags up to appear in the entertainment in place of a bearded lady. He seems rather disappointed when the show is cancelled and he has to take off the dress.

Percy: He admits to being quite moved after reading the 'tragic ancient Egyptian masterpiece' *The Death of the Pharaoh!* Whether he's similarly emotional after seeing it performed, complete with bagpipe music, is unknown.

The King: The philosophy of Richard XII of Scotland is uncomplicated and spiritual: 'Love thy neighbour as thyself unless he's Turkish – in which case, kill the bastard!' In pursuit of a good fight, he finds himself in Constantinople up against ten thousand scimitar-wielding Turks, while he himself is armed only with a small knife for peeling fruit. He is feared dead, but with odds like those it's no real surprise when he comes through it unscathed (unlike the ten thousand Turks). He thinks his son is called Edward, or possibly Enid.

The Queen: Gertrude, Queen of Flanders, likes eunuchs a great deal; in fact she wishes she'd married one. She doesn't much care for the King making love to her: it makes her feel like the outside of a sausage roll and stops her getting to sleep. It was a different matter with 'Big Boy' Donald, whose galleon was always assured of a warm welcome in her harbour.

Prince Harry: Born in 1460, he consequently has seniority over Edmund. With the King away from home fighting until St Leonard's Day, Harry divides the resultant plethora of duties between himself and his brother. He takes care of visiting royalty, the guards of honour and papal legate, while Edmund is assigned frolics and drains. Under normal circumstances, though, it's likely that Harry would get out his plunger and see to the latter himself.

Name Checks: Bernard the Rabbit-Baiter is the star of the show as far as the Queen is concerned. Imagine how impressed she'd have been if he'd brought a bear. The Archbishop of York wants the King to join his Italian formation dancing class.

The World According to the Black Adder: Morris dancing is, in Black Adder's opinion, 'the most fatuous tenth-rate entertainment ever devised by man: forty effeminate blacksmiths waving bits of cloth they've just wiped their noses on.' If there's anyone he likes less than morris dancers, it's the Scots. Half of them, he opines, are Barbarians who can't even speak English – its all Greek to him. Not that they actually speak Greek, you understand, it just sounds like Greek. He won't miss not being able to pass laws over Scotland: in fact, he wouldn't pass water over Scotland.

Essential Knowledge: To all intents and purposes, this is a remake of the previous year's pilot episode. The plot is almost identical but, although great chunks of the dialogue remain from the original, the script has been adapted to better incorporate the revised setting and developed characters. For example: McAngus knowingly sets up Edmund; the play is always meant to be part of the entertainment rather than an impromptu addition of Edmund's; and the Jumping Jesuits have evolved into the Jumping Jews of Jerusalem (accompanied by the strains of a Jew's harp). A significant improvement indeed.

3: THE ARCHBISHOP

First Broadcast: 29 June 1983.

Herbert, Archbishop of Canterbury (Paul McDowell)
Godfrey, Archbishop of Canterbury (Arthur Hewlett)
William, Bishop of London (Arthur Hewlett)
Mother Superior (Joyce Grant)
Sister Sara (Carolyn Colquohoun)
Duke of Westminster (Russell Enoch)
Cain, a Peasant (Bert Parnaby)
Abel, a Peasant (Roy Evans)
Sir Justin de Boinod (Bill Wallis)
Sir George de Boeuf (David Delve)
Lord Graveney (Leslie Sands)

1487: fear of eternal damnation is inducing dying lords to bequeath their lands to the Church rather than the Crown; Richard is not a happy King. Not too coincidentally, the Archbishop of Canterbury dies horribly (that's the third this year) and Edmund is delighted by the rumour that Prince Harry is to be the next incumbent. The King does indeed hand the Holy Seal of Canterbury to his son, but he chooses the one whom he's always despised. Soon, the Black Adder's guile is put to the test, as he persuades the fading Lord Graveney that the Church doesn't need his land and that Hell isn't such a bad place. For once, Richard appreciates his son, who in turn looks forward to making extra cash by selling holy relics and pimping for nuns. Unfortunately, two knights mishear the King recounting the tale of Henry II and Thomas à Becket, and think he wants rid of a turbulent priest. Edmund, Percy and Baldrick are pursued into the nunnery, where all concerned disguise themselves with nun's habits before beginning a fight – which is interrupted by the Mother Superior. Edmund is less than devastated to find himself excommunicated from the Church, by all three Popes.

Watch Out For: Russell Enoch, more often known throughout his acting career as William Russell, was used to acting in a historical setting, having been TV's *Sir Lancelot* (Britain's first ever colour series, no less). He also travelled about in time as Ian Chesterton in the early *Doctor Who*s. And, in the more contemporary setting of *Coronation Street*, he played Rita's ill-fated husband Ted Sullivan.

Cunning Plans: Not so much cunning as desperate, Edmund plans to flee to France rather than go to Canterbury.

You Horrid Little Man: Edmund forces Percy to rub his face in some dung.

Double Entendres: If he fails in his duty as the Archbishop of Canterbury, Edmund the Unwilling risks facing the same treatment from his father as God meted out on the Sodomites. He doesn't know what that is but, as Baldrick points out, it can't be any worse than what the Sodomites did to each other.

Suspiciously Modern: The merchandise made in Jesus's carpentry shop (well, by Baldrick) anticipates upcoming demand and includes pipe racks, coffee tables and bookends.

Prince Edmund: Convinced that his brother is going to be the next Archbishop (virtually a death sentence), Edmund wants to look his best for the ceremony and dons his most splendid clobber: the plumed Trojan hat, the Italian shoes with the lengthy toes, and last but certainly not least the Black Russian codpiece – so big it can cause those of a sensitive nature to faint. As Primate of all England, the Black Adder has to wear purple. He packs the dwarf to take to Canterbury with him and tries on Joan of Arc's tits when he thinks no one's looking.

Baldrick: Replacing his tabard-with-snake-motif with the simple robes of a monk and partly shaving his head, Brother Baldrick takes to the ecclesiastic life like a duck to water. In next to no time he's sussed out the four main profit areas: curses (which don't work), relics (none of them genuine, not even Joan of Arc's breasts), pardons and selling the sexual favours of nuns (foreign businessmen and other nuns are the biggest clients). He also finds a novel use for a crucifix, when he whacks the Bishop of London over the head with it. Along with Edmund and Percy, he disguises himself as a nun.

Percy: Though you wouldn't think it to look at him, he is capable of sticking the boot in at the behest of his friend Edmund. For once he is considered fashionable: the peasants Cain and Abel think the manure on his face is stylish. He is quite perturbed by Baldrick's dealing in fake relics, mainly because he's just bought a 'real' bone from the finger of our Lord, for thirty-one pieces of silver off the verger. He could have got a box of ten for a groat from Baldrick, or even splashed out on a sacred appendage compendium party pack. Percy, who takes on the title of Bishop of Ramsgate, is quite slow on the uptake – he fails to realise what the two sword-wielding knights are about, even when they've all but admitted that they've come to murder the Archbishop.

The King: He makes no secret of his differing feelings for his two sons. He considers Edwin – or Egbert – excrement in comparison to Harry's cream. Richard is not a big fan of the Church, believing that it needs a good thrashing – hence the high mortality rate among archbishops.

The Queen: She is stunned by the 'enormous nonsense' that constitutes Edmund's codpiece and finds it hard to believe that her naughty little boy has become Archbishop of Canterbury; how well she remembers the time that she had to smack his bottom for relieving himself in the font. Well, she would remember it – it was only last Thursday.

Prince Harry: He risks death play-fighting with the King. His naive faith in his father is touching: he even believes that Sir Tavis Mortimer must simply have forgotten that he was wearing a helmet with a two-foot spike on it when he rushed forward, bowing in respect, to be blessed by the most recent Archbishop. Unlike his brother, he believes in God.

Name Checks: Sir Tavis Mortimer is known to some as 'the King's hired killer'. However, there's no evidence to suggest that he was culpable for the falling gargoyle that landed on Archbishop Bertram while he was swimming off Beachy Head, nor for the tragic accident in which Archbishop Wilfred somehow managed to fall on to the spire of Norwich Cathedral. Jane Smart is a bit of a gossip: it was she who told

Baldrick about the Duke and Duchess of Kent and the chocolate chastity belt. In fact there are a lot of rumours circulating: the Duchess of Gloucester is alleged to have given birth to twin goblins; Lord Wilders has a sheep in his bedroom; and as for the nuns of Uppingham and the candelabra . . .

The Next World According to the Black Adder: 'Heaven' he explains 'is for people who like the sort of things that go on in Heaven' – examples of which are 'singing, talking to God and watering pot plants.' Hell, however, apparently isn't as bad as its traditional reputation suggests. Rather than it being a place where the softest bits of your nether regions end up on the lunch menu, it is a place for people interested in the sort of pastimes that don't go on in Heaven: adultery, pillage, torture, that kind of thing.

Essential Knowledge: Although it occurred, ooh, ages ago, the assassination of Thomas à Becket has been a continuing inspiration for dramatists, from T S Eliot's *Murder in the Cathedral* to Paul Corcoran's more recent *Four Nights in Knaresborough*, a play, with more than a touch of *Blackadder* influence in evidence in which the Archbishop of Canterbury is denounced as 'a complete and utter fuckwit.'

4: THE QUEEN OF SPAIN'S BEARD

First Broadcast: 22 June 1983 (originally shown out of sequence as the second episode).

Infanta Maria Escalosa of Spain (Miriam Margolyes)
Don Speekingleesh, an Interpreter (Jim Broadbent)
Mrs Applebottom (Jane Freeman)
Revd Lloyd (John Rapley)
Mr Applebottom (Howard Lew Lewis)
Lord Chiswick (Stephen Tate)
1st Messenger (Ken Wells)
2nd Messenger (Richard Mitcheley)
3rd & 4th Messengers (David Nunn)

Archbishop (Willoughby Goddard)
Princess Leia of Hungary (Natasha King)
Lady on Ramparts (Harriet Keevil)

1492: after the collapse of the Treaty of Insects, Europe is a mess. To strengthen England's ties with Spain, a royal wedding is needed. Prince Harry's many fiancées mean he is unable to help, so Edmund is commanded to marry the Infanta Maria Escalosa. As he's not had much luck with the ladies lately, he's happy to get spliced to a beautiful princess. But then he meets her. Edmund's camping it up in outrageously effeminate clothing doesn't put off the Infanta; she's simply flattered that he's dressed as a Spanish man for her. Getting married to the peasant Tully Applebottom doesn't help either, not least because she's already married to Thomas Applebottom. There is but one hope: Maria must lose her virginity, and Baldrick is selected to undertake the possible suicide mission. But even that fails to halt the wedding: only one of the happy couple has to be a virgin. Suddenly, there's a change in Europe's balance of power. Edmund is thankful to be relieved of his obligation to Maria, and fortunately Harry has a spare Hungarian princess. Edmund's new bride-to-be is Princess Leia – who must be all of ten years old.

Watch Out For: David Nunn, last seen in 'Born to Be King', reprises his role as a messenger, which virtually makes him a semi-regular. Miriam Margolyes and Jim Broadbent would eventually reprise their double act in two arguably more important *Blackadder* roles.

Cunning Plans: Edmund is really not keen on marrying a walrus like the Infanta, which is why he listens to Percy's plan despite the fact that it's bound to be stupid. And it is. Percy thinks Edmund can put the Infanta off by pretending to be mad and getting disguised as a pig. However – and this is the cunning part – instead of going 'oink', he should go 'moo'. Our heroes' plan to rob Infanta Maria of her virginity is doomed to failure, as someone's already beaten them to it.

Cutting Comments: Edmund informs Percy that he is as much use to him as a hole in the head, 'an affliction with which you must be familiar, never having had a brain.' The Queen compares her son and the Infanta to two lovebirds, which prompts Edmund to correct her: 'One lovebird and one love elephant!'

You Horrid Little Man: Tired of listening to the interpreter 'wittering away like a pox-ridden parakeet', not to mention thinking that the man is trying to pick him up, the Black Adder punches him in the face.

Double Entendres: Not really a double entendre because it's not verbal, but, having left Edmund and Percy to practise being gay together, Baldrick returns in the middle of a violent fight and assumes that they're just throwing themselves into their roles. Harry's speech at the wedding is supposed to have a fruity theme ('It is with exstrawberry pleasure . . . may you be the apple of your husband's eyes . . . may he in turn cherries you,' etc.) and he hopes to squeeze in a banana by the end of the day.

Suspiciously Modern: Can't think why, but the name Princess Leia evokes images of robots, outer-space dogfights and hairstyles inspired by bakery products. Had the final version of Harry's fruit-based speech actually included a banana reference then, up until quite recently, it would have been considered prophetic.

Prince Edmund: He claims to have love bites on his neck, but they're really dog bites (he got pushed off a balcony by a woman because she thought he was 'so hideously ugly' and savaged by a dog). He claims to be done with the opposite sex. In his own imagination the Black Adder 'is a venomous reptile and women are his prey'. The sad truth is that women don't usually have any time for him, and he's still a virgin. What he really likes in bed is hot milk with a little cinnamon, and he prefers the company of men (Percy and Baldrick, for example), though not in an intimate sense, obviously. He resolves never to look at another woman again, but that quickly changes when he hears that he's to marry a princess.

His eventual marriage to Leia doesn't improve his unfortunate condition, as bedtime fun is restricted to reading lovely stories about fairies and elves to his extremely young bride. His dwarf is back in the cage.

Baldrick: With the promise of a hero's funeral, he all but gives his life for Edmund and sleeps with the Infanta. If that wasn't sacrifice enough, he finds himself sharing the bed with her interpreter too. He survives the encounter but is left battered and bruised, and as for the long-term psychological effects . . .

Percy: Baldrick suggests that he should help Edmund practise mincing about and acting camp, but Percy's lack of tact only ends up provoking his chum into violence.

The King: Underneath all the bluster, he has a kind heart: following the death of the King of France's son, he sees to it that flowers are sent in sympathy. Of course, it was he who had the King of France's son murdered, but it's the thought that counts. The King orders Wessex to take ten thousand men and pillage Geneva. At this point the Swiss are still allies, so he gives instructions for the men to dress as Germans. He's not keen on hearing the bad news that Lord Wessex is dead, and demands to hear some good news instead. He has some very, very large toy soldiers. He thinks his son (the slimy one) is called Osmond.

The Queen: She believes that men only want one thing, and she knows what it is: bread and butter pudding with raisins in. Oh, and the other thing of course: custard.

Prince Harry: It seems he is the world's most eligible bachelor, engaged at the last count to: Princess Leia of Hungary, Grand Duchess Ursula of Brandenburgh, Queen Beowulfa of Iceland, Countess Caroline of Luxembourg, several Berthas from various lands, Jezebel of Estonia and Bernard of Saxe-Coburg. Hang on, that's wrong . . . it's Bertha of Saxe-Coburg. And Jeremy of Estonia. He's obviously not managed to meet all his fiancées yet, otherwise he wouldn't have mistaken the Infanta for the aforementioned

Jeremy. He can speak Spanish and retains his keen interest in drains.

Name Checks: One of Baldrick's plans sees Edmund adopt the style of the Earl of Doncaster, a 'steaming great left-footer' and a special friend of the Duke of Beaufort. He does rather too good a job of it: his own father mistakes him for Doncaster himself. Strangely enough, the Russian royal family have not been 'mistaken for bison due to their excessive winter clothing and hunted down, chopped to pieces and eaten as little sweets by Mongolian bandits' so the king's guess was wide of the mark really.

Essential Knowledge: The famous blue stone of Galveston is a famous blue stone, and it comes from Galveston. By repute, it's slightly less blue than the Infanta's eyes – although, having seen neither, Percy wouldn't really know.

5: WITCHSMELLER PURSUIVANT

First Broadcast: 13 July 1983.

The Witchsmeller Pursuivant (Frank Finlay)
Ross, a Lord (Richard Murdoch)
Angus, a Lord (Valentine Dyall)
Rife, a Lord (Peter Schofield)
Princess Leia of Hungary (Natasha King)
Soft, a Guard (Stephen Frost)
Anon, a Guard (Mark Arden)
Daft Red, a Peasant (Perry Benson)
Dim Cain (Bert Parnaby)
Dumb Abel (Roy Evans)
Dopey Jack (Forbes Collins)
Officer, an Officer (Patrick Duncan)
Jane Firkettle (Barbara Miller)
Piers, a Yeoman (Howard Lew Lewis)
Mrs Field, a Goodwife (Sarah Thomas)
Mrs Tyler, a Goodwife (Louise Gold)
Stuntman (Gareth Milne)

Murdered Lord (John Carlisle)
Trusting Father (Forbes Collins).

1495: the Black Plague is ravaging Europe, and not even eating rats can halt its deadly spread. Who do you call when the King appears to be possessed and weird happenings are observed throughout the land? The Witchsmeller Pursuivant, that's who. Edmund is curious about him, and thinks Mistress Scott the crone might provide some information. And well she might have done, had the Witchsmeller not burnt her at the stake. Next up, 'Old Big Nose' intends to sniff out the chief witch – who, unsurprisingly, turns out to be the one man daft enough to have insulted him. Edmund's badly chosen comments, not to mention his haircut, serve to land him deeper and deeper in it, and Percy and Baldrick are guilty by association. Even a daring escape from their trial can't save them. On the verge of being burnt alive for being Grumbledook, brother of Lucifer, a desperate Black Adder turns to his mother for help. But there is no last-minute reprieve; the Queen can only send Edmund's young wife with a dolly to comfort him. Edmund, Percy and Baldrick prepare to become a sizzling supper for Satan. But, as the flames touch the Queen's doll, the Witchsmeller is consumed by fire. Seems there was a witch on the premises after all . . .

Watch Out For: A mixed bag, this episode. Alternative comedy duo Stephen Frost and Mark Arden appear, as does half of a comedy duo from an earlier generation: Richard 'Stinker' Murdoch, erstwhile partner of 'Big Hearted' Arthur Askey. There's also a guest spot for Valentine Dyall who was the original *Man in Black* (1949). Look out as well for the demon sitting in court, you can't miss him. Veteran actor Frank Finlay is credited as a special guest star in the opening titles; he's probably best known for his title role in the BBC's *Casanova*, and for the controversial ITV drama *A Bouquet of Barbed Wire*.

Cunning Plans: Unfortunately, we don't quite hear Baldrick's most cunningly brilliant plan ever, but it works perfectly and somehow allows Edmund and the others to leap into the air in the courtroom and land in the corridor outside.

The fact that they are quickly recaptured can't diminish what must have been a first-rate plan. Conversely, the plan to escape prison by dressing up as washerwomen and get out in wicker baskets is not cunning at all, not least because the guards are obviously very familiar with that one. By the time he's tied to the stake, the Black Adder has had his fill of cunning plans – so, when Baldrick claims to have yet another, his response is, 'Oh, fuck off, Baldrick!' (OK, so someone deliberately coughs over the top of this line, but it's still pretty blatant.)

Cutting Comments: The insult 'Old Big Nose' might not be the most offensive in Edmund's repertoire – but, aimed at the wrong person, a jibe like that can have the direst consequences.

Double Entendres: Well, the Narrator's line about the Plague being spread by seamen got a big laugh from the audience.

Suspiciously Modern: The Queen appears to have studied witchcraft under the nose-twitching Samantha from the American TV series *Bewitched*. Of all the bizarre omens witnessed around the land, there was none stranger than that of the four-headed man taking tea – because tea wasn't available in England until 1657.

Prince Edmund: He isn't fooled by all the talk of omens and strange sightings: to him, a horse with two heads and two bodies is obviously two horses side by side. His own horse, by the way, is called Black Satin – or it was, until the Witchsmeller killed it. He also has a cat named Bubbles (or Beelzebubbles, as the Witchsmeller suggests). His earlier success emulating the Earl of Doncaster must have been a fluke – for not only is he no master of disguise (he tries to conceal himself among the peasants by wearing a strip of cloth over part of his face), but also he can't remember if he's supposed to be posing as Clever Jake, Clever Pete or even Clever Tom. He gets another change of appearance when, along with Percy and Baldrick, his head is shaved prior to execution. In Edmund's case, it's an improvement. He may or may not have fathered John Grumbledook, a small poodle (probably not, actually). He's still married to Leia.

Baldrick: He's not the superstitious type: he knows its rubbish to think that sticking your finger up a sheep's bottom on Good Friday makes you fertile. It only works on Easter Monday. Whichever day it is, Edmund won't be shaking his hand on a religious festival.

Percy: He and Edmund have been 'friends' since schooldays, if not longer. According to him, the land is abundant with strange happenings: phlegm raining from the skies, women raped by fish, ghosts rising from their graves to play sport – and one of Percy's friends even got a pimple inside his nose. Judging by his reaction to the small pile of ashes that had previously been Mistress Scott's moggie, he has a fondness for cats. In the absence of any actual lawyers willing to take on the task, Percy acts as Edmund's defence in court.

The King: He misses all the strange phenomena, witchcraft, hellish goings-on, etc., because he's laid up in bed, a bit off-colour with the Plague.

The Queen: She knows more about the occult than she's telling.

Prince Harry: With the King out of action, he assumes responsibility for running things. And, while he proves himself both naive and thick, he has the makings of a true King inasmuch as people take notice of what he says and, more importantly, agree with him. He's very, very quick to believe that his younger brother is a witch.

Name Checks: The Witchsmeller discovered that every single person in Taunton was having an affair with the same duck. Edmund and Percy attended the same school as John 'Stinker' Watts, who grew up to be a lawyer and refuses to come to their aid. So does Robert Wyatt of Somerset.

The World According to the Black Adder: Edmund reckons that people who claim to be dying of the Plague are simply using it as an excuse to skive off work.

Essential Knowledge: As the Lord told the children of Bednebott in the Ten Commandments of Jereboth in the

Appendix to the Apocrypha: 'Neither shall Thou eat the fruit of the tree that is known as the carrot tree.'

6: THE BLACK SEAL

First Broadcast: 20 July 1983.

Person of Unrestricted Growth (Des Webb)
Cain, a blind beggar (Bert Parnaby)
Abel, a blind beggar (Roy Evans)
Retired Morris Dancer (John Barrard)
Mad Gerald (Himself)
Pigeon Vender (Perry Benson)
Friar Bellow (Paul Brooke)
Jack Large (Big Mick)
Three-Fingered Pete (Roger Sloman)
Guy of Glastonbury (Patrick Malahide)
Sir Wilfred Death (John Hallam)
The Hawk (Patrick Allen)
Sean the Irish Bastard (Ron Cook)

1498: as is traditional on St Juniper's Day, the King bestows new honours. Prince Harry receives a hatful, but Edmund, previously Duke of Edinburgh and Warden of the Royal Privies, finds himself left only with the Privies. Replacing Percy and Baldrick with a retired morris dancer, he sets forth from the castle to enlist help in taking over the kingdom. He seeks out the six most evil men in the land, and together no one can stop them. Well, except perhaps the Hawk – and, wouldn't you know it, the morris dancer turns out to be the Hawk in disguise. Edmund is thrown into a dungeon, while the Hawk sets off to claim the throne that isn't rightfully his. But no dungeon can hold the Black Adder for long. Well it can, but fortunately his cell-mate, Mad Gerald, has fashioned a key from his own teeth. Edmund summons his band, the Black Seal, but finds that they prefer the Hawk's leadership. Putting Edmund in a complicated but lethal torture device, they set off to slaughter the rest of the royal family. But they haven't reckoned on the cunning of Baldrick and Percy, who poison their wine and save the kingdom. Only, thanks to Percy, they poison everyone else as well . . .

Watch Out For: Patrick Allen appears as the Hawk (although *The Guinness Book of Classic TV* lists him as 'the moorhen'!). Mad Gerald, who played himself, later reverted to using the name Rik Mayall, which was probably a wise career move.

Cunning Plans: The Black Adder has a simple plan, but the Black Seal don't have the patience to listen to it: they'd prefer a cunning plan. The plan, therefore, must be cunning in its simplicity. It basically involves storming the castle, capturing the King and taking control of the Kingdom. Hmm, should work out as successfully as all his other cunning plans.

Cutting Comments: Justifying his decision to dismiss Percy, Edmund explains to his erstwhile consort that he could 'bore the leggings off a village idiot', is able to 'ride a horse rather less well than another horse would' and that his 'brain would make a grain of sand look large and ungainly'. Then he gets personal: having apparently consulted the women of the Court, he informs Percy that the part of his anatomy that can't be mentioned isn't worth mentioning anyway.

You Horrid Little Man: Once he's taken over the kingdom, Edmund intends to send his family into exile for life. Yes, life. But when the other members of the Black Seal advise him to kill his parents and brother instead, he fails to voice any objection. He beats up a merchant, ties him to a tree and steals six black homing pigeons from him – well, five black pigeons and a black chicken – in order to send out messages to his motley band.

Suspiciously Modern: Edmund pre-empts Dumas when he cries 'All for one!' – although the Black Seal's answer is 'And each man for himself!'

Prince Edmund: As a child, Edmund had a deadly rival, Philip of Burgundy, who in those days was known as the Thrush. Fifteen years later, Philip is back for revenge, only now he's become the Hawk. Losing dominion over Edinburgh and sick of playing second fiddle to brother Harry, the Black Adder is finally galvanised into action in order to fulfil his destiny of becoming king. Gathering together a dirty half-dozen of really evil villains – Sir Wilfred Death, Three-Fingered Pete, Guy de Glastonbury, Sean the Irish Bastard, Friar Bellows and Jack Large – he creates the Black Seal, their motto: 'Blessed are the meek for they shall be slaughtered!' While strapped into the Hawk's torture device, Edmund gets a spike up his nethers, his ears sheared, his hands chopped off and his coddlings ground, all of which he just about manages to survive. If only the silly sod hadn't decided to try the wine to see if it was poisoned or not, he'd have been King for longer than it took to almost say it.

Baldrick: Before he found employment with Edmund, Baldrick worked as a dung gatherer – just like his father, Robin the dung gatherer. After getting sacked, he ponders the wisdom of returning to his former profession. He knows he'll have to start at the bottom again, perhaps mucking out the lepers, but maybe in a few years he'll be able to work his way up to shovelling dung. Yet again, he gets disguised as a woman. Ostensibly, this is a ruse to get the Black Seal to drink poisoned wine, but it really is becoming a habit.

Percy: If he feels hard done by getting sacked, the fact that his stupidity is responsible for causing the demise of the House of Plantagenet should reassure him that perhaps he wasn't really up to the job anyway.

The King: He plans to 'honour' Stoke by baring his broad buttocks outside the city walls. That'll be a treat for the inhabitants! Apparently the length of his rod is a mystery to all but the Queen and a thousand Turkish whores. Thanks to Percy, the length of Richard IV's reign is cut short at thirteen years. He thinks his son is called Egbert, or perhaps Edgar, the Black Dagger.

The Queen: Doesn't do much apart from get upset about Edmund's terrible mutilated condition – and die, of course.

Prince Harry: He becomes Captain of the Guard, Grand Warden of the Northern and Eastern Marches, Chief Lunatic of the Duchy of Gloucester and Sheriff of Nottingham. There are a few other titles too, but since Harry dies before he can look up any of his new lands on the map, who cares which?

Name Checks: There is some confusion about which evil villain named Jack will complete the roster of the Black Seal. Could it be Mad Bully Boy Jack, the Grave-Robbing Assassin of Aldwych? No. Then how about Crazed Animal Jack, the Cattle-Rustling Cannibal from Sutton Coldfield? Not him. Must be Sane Jack O'Hooligan, the Man-Hating Goat Murderer of Dingle Bay? It isn't, actually. Surely it can't be Canon Jack Smollett, Senior Archdeacon of the Diocese of St Wotan, the Entrail-Eating Heretic of Bath and Wells? Certainly not, so what about Unspeakably Violent Jack, the Bull-Buggering Priest-Killer of no fixed abode? Could be. Friar Bellows knows that Jolly Jasper, landlord of the tavern that will provide the rendezvous point for his partners in villainy, is dead – because he killed him!

The World According to the Black Adder: Actually, he doesn't have an opinion of it; rather a desire to rule it.

Essential Knowledge: A caption claims that Edmund spends over a year in the dungeon at the mercy of ravenous snails (another fourteen and he would have been completely devoured). However, the episode begins in 1498 and we already know that that's the year in which Richard IV's reign ends and, anyway, why would the Hawk wait for over a year to make his move? We suspect, then, that said caption was just a silly joke – so, the snail threat was never as great as it seemed.

3: BLACKADDER II

The Elizabethan Schmuck

When Prince Edmund died a lingering death, it was nearly the last we ever heard of his dynasty. Despite winning awards and building a strong cult following, *The Black Adder* was only moderately successful in terms of viewing figures. It was also expensive to make – and Michael Grade, the BBC 1 controller of the time, decided it wasn't delivering enough jokes to the pound. The series was cancelled.

And there the story might have ended, were it not for the intervention of one man.

Enter the Motormouth

Pre-*Blackadder*, Ben Elton was best known as a stand-up comedian, famous for his spangly 'Sellafield' suit, the left-wing content of his act (although the right-wing press exaggerated that) and the fast-paced delivery that earned him the nickname 'Motormouth'. Having studied drama at Manchester University (where he met Rik Mayall and Adrian Edmondson – they were on the same course, a few years further on) and put on his own play at college at the age of sixteen, he went on to write and perform his own stand-up routine in the early days of London's now-famous Comedy Store.

Here, he appeared alongside such up-and-coming young comics as Mayall and Edmondson, French and Saunders, Alexei Sayle and just about everyone else who was destined to become famous when 'alternative' comedy took over TV in the mid-80s. He eventually became the Comedy Store's regular compere, but his big break really came when Mayall asked him to help write *The Young Ones*, an anarchic sitcom that turned out to be more than a mite influential. It was also Mayall's recommendation that helped him get the post of main writer and co-star of the Granada sketch show *Alfresco*, on which, he has since confessed, he was paid to learn from his mistakes. More about that later.

It was on the strength of *The Young Ones* – and, apparently, thanks to a chance meeting – that Richard Curtis asked Elton to replace Rowan Atkinson as his *Blackadder* co-writer. 'Rowan really dropped out of writing on the first series,' Curtis told *Cult TV* magazine in 1998. 'He doesn't take any credit for it at all.' Charged with revamping the series into something that Michael Grade might actually like, Elton was more successful than anyone could have imagined. Indeed, his appointment remains arguably the most important turning point in *Blackadder*'s history.

At about the time that *Blackadder II* reached our screens, Elton was taking his stand-up routines to a larger audience via Channel 4's *Saturday Live*. The tabloids didn't like it – after all, he was poking fun at their beloved Mrs Thatcher – but, despite (or because of) them, he gained a lot of fans. And the tabloids would eventually change their minds about him, as his name became synonymous with a *Blackadder* that was about to find its feet and, from there, grow into a television phenomenon.

Today, Ben Elton prospers as an internationally bestselling novelist (*Stark, Gridlock, Blast from the Past*, etc.), a playwright, a performer and now a film director (*Maybe Baby*, 2000, adapted from his own novel, *Inconceivable*, and starring Hugh Laurie). He also gets his own BBC 1 show performing his stand-up routine every four years or so: to date, *Ben Elton – The Man From Auntie* in 1990, *The Man From Auntie* in 1994 and *The Ben Elton Show* in 1998.

First Impressions

If there's one thing that, on first viewing, sets *Blackadder II* apart from its predecessor, it's that it was much cheaper to make – and it shows!

The change is obvious right from the opening titles: the panoramic views of Alnwick Castle and its snow-covered surroundings are replaced by a single close-up shot of a snake slithering across a table, with black-gloved hands entering the picture at intervals to steer it back on course. Howard Goodall's original strident, action-adventure theme is replaced by a more appropriately laid-back mock-madrigal arrangement.

It was Ben Elton, apparently, who pointed out to Richard Curtis that *The Black Adder* could have been made as a traditional, in-studio, thirty-minute sitcom, bereft of its lavish location work and with the action mostly confined to a few regular sets. In fact, he thought it could actually have been funnier that way. 'Rowan falling off a horse at two hundred metres is not really any funnier than anyone else falling off a horse at two hundred metres,' he told the BBC series *Laughter in the House: The Story of British Sitcom* in 1999, 'but get the camera in close and he'll make you laugh.'

Curtis and Elton revamped the format accordingly, and the accountants' eyes must have lit up when they saw their plan. Satisfied that each joke would now cost significantly less, Michael Grade gave the go-ahead to an almost entirely studiobound *Blackadder II*. The first episode, 'Bells', finally aired on 9 January 1986, an almost unprecedented two and a half years after 'The Black Seal'.

Ironically, the end result resembles nothing more than the pilot episode of *The Black Adder*, not least because Curtis decided to return to his original idea of an Elizabethan setting (this time, no dates are given on-screen, but publicity material refers to the six episodes as taking place during 1560, 1561, 1562, 1564, 1565 and 1566 respectively). Where it differs is that the writers had to abandon the epic storylines that had been such an integral part of Curtis and Atkinson's original concept: the pilot was obviously a cheap programme trying to tell an expensive story, and *Blackadder II* could only avoid this pitfall by narrowing its scope.

To regular viewers, then, the new series was something of a shock. Anyone expecting the further grandiose, history-shaking exploits of the villainous, power-hungry Prince Edmund was surprised to witness instead the rather more domestic affairs of his less ambitious descendant. Edmund Blackadder hardly even left his house, unless it was to pop across to Richmond for a quick chat with the Queen of England.

By all rights, *Blackadder II* should have been a pale imitation of its predecessor, and a colossal disaster. But, to this day, it possesses something that the majority of television comedies lack: it's funny. In fact, it's very funny indeed. Transvestite manservants, comedy breasts, baby-eating bishops, turnips that are exactly the same shape as thingies . . . these things have all entered the nation's collective comic consciousness (excuse us for using a poncey phrase, but you know what we mean).

You see, Ben Elton was right. Money doesn't buy laughs. But the combination of Curtis and Elton – each working separately, before swapping scenes to check over and add to what the other had written – provided lots of them. Even Atkinson thought the new scripts were better, as he told *Radio Times*: 'I'm actually happier with this series and believe it has wider appeal. It's more zappy and anarchic.'

The presence of a live studio audience was probably an improvement, too. Well, we assume it would have been, else why do most comedy shows have one? Actors often feel 'lifted' by the atmosphere on set, and can time their performances around the laughter. This is particularly noticeable in the final episode of the series, 'Chains'.

Blackadder II isn't the complete break from its predecessor that, superficially, it appears to be. The cunning plans are still there, as are the cutting comments, the double entendres and the suspiciously modern references, as our episode guide attests. Some changes, though, do run deep. Nowadays, we're well used to seeing different takes upon the characters of Blackadder and Baldrick. However, it was their reinterpretation for *Blackadder II* that would provide the template for every descendant of the pair that followed.

Out of the Melting Pot

'The filthy genes of the Blackadder family have resurfaced in the melting pot of history.' So the press release for

Blackadder II has it. Edmund Blackadder, apparently, is the bastard great-great-grandson of Prince Edmund – although just when the latter spread his seed and when his *nom de plume* was adopted as a family name is left unexplained. In fact, there is no mention of Blackadder's ancestry in the episodes themselves; only the song that accompanies the closing credits of 'Head' makes reference to it ('His great grandfather was a king'), and even that drops one 'great' in order to scan correctly.

Television critics love to comment on Rowan Atkinson's 'rubbery features' – and, with the addition of a beard and a less 'nerdish' haircut, he presents a character who, in appearance and mannerisms, is very different to Prince Edmund, Duke of Edinburgh (but, again, suspiciously similar to Prince Edmund, Duke of York).

The character's IQ has leapt up a few points, too. No longer is he an object of ridicule; rather, it is he who does the ridiculing, often appearing to be the only person around with any intelligence. His comments are usually barbed, but they're also clever and witty, and, let's face it, we'd all like to have had the brains and the bottle to make them ourselves. He's still cruel and amoral, but his evil streak is much less pronounced and, anyway, he's more charming with it. This, then, was the new Blackadder – and it says a lot for Atkinson's versatility that it's hard to equate this handsome, debonair, likeable rogue with the vile, ugly villain who apparently spawned him.

Ben Elton has claimed that one of his favourite lines from *Blackadder II* comes from the first episode, 'Bells', as an irritated Blackadder corrects a young crone's use of language ('"Yes it is", not "that it be"!'). We'd have gone for the ear-muffs joke in 'Beer', ourselves – but Elton's choice illustrates another key facet of the character: that he's hardly an Elizabethan gentleman at all, but rather a modern-day man with modern-day sensibilities, transposed to Elizabethan times. This is just one more reason why, despite his sometimes despicable acts, we can identify with Edmund Blackadder in a way that we couldn't with Prince Edmund. And that's probably why, despite being less obviously a figure of fun, he proved to be a more successful comic creation.

Somehow latching on to Blackadder, as their ancestors once did to his, are Percy and Baldrick. Percy – Lord Percy Percy in this incarnation – is . . . well, he's just Percy. Still stupid, still vain, still hoping to benefit from Blackadder's reflected glory (although their status is more equal in this era – they both have the title Lord – it is Blackadder who has the ear of the Queen – not literally, of course, 'cos that would just be horrible).

If Percy hasn't changed, though, then Baldrick certainly has. Curtis and Elton compensated for Blackadder's increased brain power by giving his servant a measure of intelligence somewhere below that of a dung beetle. 'Baldrick is an example of regressive evolution,' Tony Robinson told the *Radio Times* in 1989. 'In the first series, his cunning plans were better than everybody else's. By the second series, he was on his way down. By 2000 AD he will be an amoeba.' A less than accurate prophecy, given that by 2000 AD Baldrick would be busy building time machines – but the rest of the statement is perfectly true.

A Whole New Gang of Idiots

Less a rewriting of history than an adjunct to it, *Blackadder II* emulates its predecessor by making a regular character of the English monarch, but differs from it in plumping for a monarch who actually existed. Of Queen Elizabeth I – 'Good Queen Bess' as she became known – the *Encyclopaedia Britannica* notes that she 'transformed herself into a powerful image of female authority, regal magnificence and national pride, and that image has endured to the present.' If it has, then it's no thanks to Miranda Richardson's magnificent portrayal of 'Queenie' as a self-obsessed, excitable, unpredictable, overgrown child.

Prior to *Blackadder*, Richardson was a respected stage actor, although she was probably best known for her very serious screen role as another historical character, Ruth Ellis, the last woman to be hanged in England, in the 1985 film *Dance With a Stranger*. She had already dabbled in TV comedy, with guest appearances in a few episodes of *Alas Smith and Jones*. Since *Blackadder*, though, she has gone on to bigger things, appearing in more films than we can comfortably list here. Her many TV drama credits include *Merlin* (as both Queen Mab and her sister, the Lady of the Lake), *Alice in Wonderland* (as the Queen of Hearts), *The Scold's Bridle* and *A Dance to the Music of Time* (not as any sort of queen at all). She's very much in demand for comedy appearances: she joined the Comic Strip team when they reformed for a few new episodes of *The Comic Strip Presents* in the nineties, guest starred in *Absolutely Fabulous* and appeared in *Ted and Ralph*, a spin-off from *The Fast Show*.

At Queen Elizabeth's court, she was joined by Patsy Byrne in the role of Queenie's nursemaid. Byrne's screen career has seen her play quite a lot of nurses, matrons and the like – from a television production of *Romeo and Juliet* (1976) to *Britannia Hospital* (1982) and 1990 TV movie *The Silver Chair*, in which she played a giant nanny – but Nursie (or, to give her her proper name, Bernard) was probably the most stupid.

Two more additions to the *Blackadder* team came in the persons of Stephen Fry and Hugh Laurie (we've lumped them together because they're best known as a double act). Having taken part in the 1981 Cambridge Footlights Revue, they graduated to *Alfresco* (see, we told you we'd get back to it) along with fellow Footlighter Emma Thompson, Siobhan Redmond and, eventually, *Blackadder* guest-star-to-be Robbie Coltrane (all three destined for bigger and more dramatic things, as were Fry and Laurie themselves).

Fry appeared throughout *Blackadder II* as the Queen's trouble-making religious advisor and Blackadder's bitter rival, Lord Melchett – while Laurie only guest starred, albeit as different characters in two consecutive episodes (the inebriated Simon Partridge in 'Beer' and the scheming Prince Ludwig in 'Chains'). However, both would go on to play very prominent parts in future *Blackadder* series before writing and starring in the popular sketch show *A Bit of Fry and Laurie*, which ran for four seasons between 1989 and 1995 (after a pilot episode in 1986); they would also take the title roles in four seasons of *Jeeves and Wooster* (Fry was Jeeves) in the early nineties.

The first episode of the series, 'Bells', also introduced a pair of characters who, though not intended as regulars, were so memorable that they would eventually return.

Blackadder's surprisingly feminine manservant, Bob, was played by Gabrielle Glaister. Nowadays, she is best known for having survived seven years in *Brookside*, as middle-class mother-of-two Patricia Farnham, without being blown up, losing any children or living through a gun siege. Co-incidentally, Glaister was at school with Ben Elton: her very first acting role was as Oliver in a school production, in which Elton played the Artful Dodger. And, before anyone cries 'nepotism', it *was* a coincidence. She got the role of Bob when she was spotted in the stage show *Daisy Pulls It Off*.

Bob, you will recall, revealed that her real name was Kate, and agreed to marry Blackadder, only to run off with his best man at the wedding. The despicable but irresistible Lord Flashheart was played by another old chum of Elton's, Rik Mayall.

We've already mentioned Mayall several times, but suffice it to say that he made his name with *The Young Ones* and has since perfected the format with *Bottom*, via another Elton-scripted series, *Filthy, Rich and Catflap*. He has also proved himself as a serious actor, and is well remembered for his role as Conservative MP Alan B'Stard, alias *The New Statesman*. Flashheart was actually Mayall's second *Blackadder* character: he appeared as Mad Gerald in 'The Black Seal', although he wasn't credited (the credits claimed that Gerald had, in fact, played himself; something that he had in common with one of Mayall's earliest TV characters, incompetent journalist Kevin Turvey).

Another regular character remains uncredited. The series' closing titles, shot on location (along with just one scene from 'Bells'), show Blackadder making his way along a bush-lined path, to be harassed in a variety of ways by a bal-ladeer who has set his most recent experiences to music (the series' theme, to be exact). The lyrics to each song were worked out 'over a pint' by Richard Curtis, Ben Elton and

Howard Goodall. 'That was always the fun of *Blackadder*,' Goodall told Fleetway's *Red Dwarf Smegazine* in 1992, 'doing more and more ridiculous lyrics that had less and less to do with the programme.'

Terribly Pedantic Bit About Episode Order

There is plenty of evidence to suggest that 'Head' was originally to have been transmitted first, with 'Bells' second, rather than vice versa:

a) Percy has a beard in 'Head'. He shaves it off halfway through 'Bells' and is bereft of it for the rest of the series.
b) Queenie wears her hair up in 'Head', and throughout 'Bells' until Flashheart tells her he prefers it down. She wears it that way thereafter.
c) The song at the end of 'Head' sets the scene for the entire series, noting that 'His great grandfather was a king, Although for only thirty seconds.'
d) Even during the week that 'Bells' was transmitted, the *Radio Times* was still referring to Rik Mayall's appearance (as Flashheart) in the *second* episode. The *Guardian*, though noting that episode one was called 'Bells', described the plot of 'Head', presumably quoting from an earlier press release.

So, pretty conclusive then, we think. Anyway, 'Bells' is a better episode than 'Head', and also Ben Elton's personal favourite, so it seems likely that the switch was pulled to give the series a stronger start. However, unlike the earlier transposition of 'Born to be King' and 'The Queen of Spain's Beard', it has never been reversed. All video releases, repeat seasons, etc., have stuck to the order of the original broadcast – which is why we've also kept that order in our episode guide, despite the discrepancies.

On the subject of such trivia, you might care to know why *Blackadder II* wasn't broadcast on the night of Thursday 30 January 1986. It was dropped to make way for the BBC's then-quite-new quarterly crime-busting show, *Crimewatch UK*.

And Then They All Died – Again!

Few people could claim not to have been prepared. Advance publicity for the episode 'Chains', as quoted in the *Radio Times* and other listings, described it thus: 'Very funny last episode in which the court get horribly murdered at the end again.'

With hindsight, there's not even much reason why the court *should* have been horribly murdered. While *The Black Adder* had presented itself as a forgotten chapter in history, and therefore had to present a conclusion to said chapter, *Blackadder II* had successfully reinvented itself as a traditional sitcom that hardly challenged our view of history at all. Still, Curtis and Elton felt that the tale of Edmund Blackadder should reach a definite conclusion, and so a murderous finale it was.

'Chains' is the one episode of *Blackadder II* that most resembles its predecessor, given that it revolves around a plot to overthrow the British throne. Even so, the story of the evil German Prince Ludwig and his grand machinations pretty much boils down to a few scenes of Blackadder and Melchett sitting in a dungeon. Curtis and Elton play towards the viewers' carefully built expectation of a tragic finale by having Blackadder save the day at the last minute. Then, in a cursory post-credits scene, we learn that Ludwig has somehow taken on the identity of Elizabeth and slaughtered the real queen, along with everyone else. Less a dramatic finale than an opportunistic punch line, really.

But even this isn't such a drastic rewrite of history as it might seem. Although Ludwig presumably ruled, as Elizabeth, for another thirty-seven years, he/she had no direct descendants (well, that would have been a bit difficult to explain, wouldn't it?) and power thus passed to the first Stuart king, James VI of Scotland, upon his/her death.

It wasn't until a few years later that Germans really took over the British throne . . .

What the Papers Said

Blackadder II was a much more popular and influential series than its predecessor. The format, characters and dialogue of all future reincarnations of the *Blackadder* format would owe a lot more to the antics of Edmund Blackadder than to the exploits of Prince Edmund. It's no overstatement, then, to say that *Blackadder II* is one of the most important comedy series ever shown on British television. So, surely those great makers of opinion, the TV critics, had much to say in the wake of its trailblazing arrival upon our screens?

Well, actually, no. You see, 'Bells' first aired at 9.30 p.m. on a Thursday evening on BBC 1. It was immediately preceded, on BBC 2, by another comedy series returning with a new name. And, as *Yes, Minister* had been a bit more successful than *The Black Adder*, it was *Yes, Prime Minister* not *Blackadder II* that got all the attention.

Not that *Blackadder II* was totally ignored. The *Daily Mail* described it as a 'promising new series', although their writer had a bee in his bonnet about laughter tracks (whether real or canned) being used in this and other shows.

For the *Daily Telegraph*, Ronald Hastings delivered what can only be described as a backhanded compliment: 'The first series was so variable, all right, so awful, that the BBC must have been reluctant to make a second. It is good that they did, for this is a great improvement.' He went on to praise the actors for 'avoiding excesses, apart from Rik Mayall, who has to be excused as excess for him is moderation.' However, he did warn that the script was 'sometimes not of surpassing cleanliness.' Scathing words indeed.

'This is sitcom at its most thrillingly historical,' commented *Potato Quarterly* on the episode 'Potato'. However, as *Potato Quarterly* was a made-up publication, quoted in jest in the *Radio Times*, it doesn't count.

The most substantial – and funniest – review, however, comes from Maureen Patton in the *Daily Express*. She accused 'Bells' of being 'completely obsessed with people's naughty bits', with scenes being 'ruined by the schoolboy shock-tactic of spelling things out.' Miranda Richardson, she said, 'made an exceptionally silly, screechy Queen Elizabeth I, who should never have been let out of her playpen.'

When *Blackadder II* was released on video a few years later, the writers of the back cover blurb had the cheek to quote out of context Patton's admission that 'There were some amusing lines in the first episode'. Since the series was, by then, assured of both enduring popularity and a place in history, they probably felt that its video sales could survive such a less-than-ringing endorsement.

Blackadder II

Edmund Blackadder (Rowan Atkinson)
Lord Percy (Tim McInnerny)
Baldrick (Tony Robinson)
Queen Elizabeth I (Miranda Richardson)
Lord Melchett (Stephen Fry)
Nursie (Patsy Byrne)

Written by Richard Curtis and Ben Elton; directed by
Mandie Fletcher; produced by John Lloyd.

1: BELLS

First Broadcast: 9 January 1986.

Kate (Gabrielle Glaister)
Flashheart (Rik Mayall)
Dr Leech (John Grillo)
Kate's Father (Edward Jewesbury)
Wisewoman (Barbara Miller)
Young Crone (Sadie Shimmin)

Kate's family is penniless. Despite her father's wish for her to
become a prostitute, she makes for London, disguises herself
as a boy and seeks a servant's wage in the house of Blackadder. Blackadder tries to deny his affection for the mysterious 'Bob' – after all, he is a chap – but he's soon giving
him flowers and almost kissing him. His doctor's plan to cure
his apparent homosexuality with leeches fails, as does

Baldrick's suggestion of travelling to 1 Dunghill Mansions, Putney, and consulting the wisewoman. However, when Bob shows Blackadder what 'he' keeps in his tights, all is made right. A wedding is arranged, with Baldrick standing in as bridesmaid as Kate is too poor to afford actual friends. The best man is to be an old schoolchum of Blackadder's, the adventurer Lord Flashheart. The only hitch is that Kate's father smells of cabbages and has to be persuaded to leave with a tenner. Oh, and Flashheart and Kate run away together, having swapped costumes because Kate has grown to like boys' clothes and Flash has always felt more comfy in a dress. On these occasions, it's customary for the jilted groom to marry the bridesmaid . . .

Watch Out For: The wisewoman could be a descendant of Regan, one of the three witches in 'The Foretelling' – although another potential ancestor, Jane Firkettle, was on the side of the prosecution in 'Witchsmeller Pursuivant'.

Cunning Plans: The wisewoman offers Blackadder 'three cunning plans to cure thy ailment'. He can kill Bob, kill himself or make sure that no one ever knows about them by killing everybody else. So, now we know where Baldrick gets it from.

Cutting Comments: For once, Blackadder is on the receiving end, as Dr Leech tells him: 'It's not every day a man wakes up to discover he's a screaming bender with no more right to live on God's clean earth than a weasel.' Accused of being a quack, he responds: 'I'd rather be a quack than a ducky.' Referring to Baldrick as a 'man', Blackadder notes: 'I use the word "man" in its broadest possible sense – for as we all know, God made man in his own image. It'd be a sad lookout for Christians throughout the globe if God looked anything like you, Baldrick.' And Baldrick the bridesmaid 'looks like what he is: a dungball in a dress.'

You Horrid Little Man: Baldrick has to hold up a target for Blackadder's archery practice (which results in Percy's arrow accidentally entering Baldrick's willy). Percy is made to reveal all about Jane Harrington with two kicks to the testicles. Blackadder thinks nothing of throwing Baldrick out on to the street

– in fact, he has tried to kill him in the past. He threatens a young crone with a 'wild stab in the dark', and plans to get his ten pounds back by having Baldrick beat up Kate's father.

Double Entendres: Kate's father pleads with her to go on the game because 'it's a steady job and you'd be working from home . . . Why walk all the way to London when you can make a fortune lying on your back?' Blackadder looks forward to having Bob (to stay, that is), and Percy likes him because he's got balls. Hearing that Blackadder has a problem with his manservant, Dr Leech advises him to pop it on the table. Flashheart is late for the wedding, and everyone wonders where he's been. 'Where *haven't* I been?!'

Suspiciously Modern: The growing relationship between Blackadder and Bob is presented in the form of a mock advert for an album of Elizabethan love songs, which includes *My Love is a Prick (on a Tudor Rose)* and *Hot Sex Madrigal in the Middle of My Tights.* Blackadder corrects a young crone's use of the phrase 'that it be' to 'yes it is'.

Blackadder: He wears his ancestor's snake-and-sword motif on his sleeve. Talk of 'rumpy-pumpy' embarrasses him, and he assumes that such a discussion with Bob would be part of 'a big lads' joke about back-ticklers'. He asserts his manhood by suggesting they get ratted, talk about girls and sing dirty songs. The wisewoman refers to him as Edmund, Lord of Adders Black, and accuses him of plotting to become King. She must be thinking of his ancestor. Had Kate revealed her true gender from the offset, she says, 'you would have just used me and cast me aside like you have so many women before,' and Blackadder seems to admit this.

Baldrick: Word has it that he's the worst servant in London. He has been in Blackadder's service since he was two and a half, which is probably why his master is so sick of the sight of him. Thrown out of the house, he lives in the gutter until the town bailiff warns him that he'll be 'flushed into the Thames with all the other turds.' He doesn't hold with 'new-fangled doctoring', preferring to take his problems to the wisewoman.

Percy: Blackadder refers to him as Peabrain, 'a dimwit I can't seem to be able to shake off.' Percy boasts of his prowess with a bow and his ability to withstand torture, but demonstrates neither. He has just lost one Jane Harrington to an unnamed Spaniard, so, upon hearing that she has a thing about beards, he shaves. Even so, he can't help but romance the next person he sees in a dress – which, unfortunately, is Baldrick. He tries to ingratiate himself with Bob by offering jolly, rosy-cheeked capers, but comes across as a creep. He wants nothing more than Blackadder's respect and friendship; he cries when the job of best man goes to Flashheart, but still takes a ring to the wedding in case there's a last-minute change of plan (but loses it when there is).

Queenie: Her father used to laugh at 'those people with the funny faces and the bells'. No, not jesters – lepers. When Elizabeth was born, everyone thought she was a boy without a winkle, until, according to Nursie, 'Sir Thomas More pointed out that a boy without a winkle is a girl, and everyone was really disappointed.' Upon hearing that Blackadder is to marry, the Queen needs to know that Kate's nose isn't as pretty as hers, 'because otherwise I would have cut it off . . . imagine the mess when she got a cold!' 'Everyone seems to get married except me,' she laments later – but at least she can get squiffy at the wedding reception and seduce someone. She has a crush on Flashheart, and lets him rearrange her hair.

Melchett: He has been in the service of the palace since the days of Queen Elizabeth's father. Apparently, Henry VIII used to be very amused by his impression of Columbus.

Nursie: She was present for the Queen's birth. Queenie has got this far in life without realising that her nursemaid's name isn't Nursie. It's Bernard. She has three sisters: Donald, Eric and Basil.

Name Checks: Jane 'Bury Me in a Y-Shaped Coffin' Harrington is tall, blonde, elegant and goes like a privy door when the plague's in town; she has broken the hearts of Blackadder, Baldrick and now Percy. Mrs Miggins's Pie Shop gets its first mention. The humble leech comes highly recommended to sixteenth-century medical practitioners by Doctor Hoffman of Stuttgart – the owner of Europe's biggest leech farm.

The World According to Lord Blackadder: He rails against 'modern' medicine, noting that 'I've never had anything you doctors didn't try to cure with leeches.'

Essential Knowledge: Two things we must know of the wisewoman. First: she is a woman. You can probably guess the second.

2: HEAD

First Broadcast: 16 January 1986.

Lady Farrow (Holly de Jong)
Gaoler Ploppy (Bill Wallis)
Mrs Ploppy (Linda Polan)
Earl Farrow (Patrick Duncan)

An opening is created when the Lord High Executioner accidentally puts his name on the wrong line of a death warrant. A reluctant Blackadder takes over, with Baldrick as his axeman. But his decision to give himself a day off by bringing forward the beheading of one James Farrow turns out to be a bit of a *faux pas*. The queen grants permission for Lady Farrow to visit her husband, so there's only one thing for it: Baldrick will have to put a bag over his head and pretend to be the dead man. Only Farrow was much taller than Baldrick, so Blackadder has to do the job himself – and even he has one arm too many. Lady Farrow, remarkably, is fooled by the impression – but then, Farrow's brother petitions the Queen and wins a pardon. Hurriedly retrieving Farrow's head from Traitors' Cloister before the Queen can see it, Blackadder is desperate enough to actually try one of Percy's plans. Fortunately, that proves unnecessary, for it transpires that Baldrick killed the wrong man anyway. Unfortunately, the Queen is on her way to see the man he *did* kill! The bag is hurriedly pressed back into service.

Watch Out For: Bill Wallis played Sir Justin de Boinod, a drunken knight freshly returned from the Crusades, in 'The Archbishop'. Patrick Duncan was an officer of the court in 'Witchsmeller Pursuivant'.

Cunning Plans: Blackadder concocts a 'cunningly plausible excuse' for the presence of a bag on 'Lord Farrow's' head. He tells Lady Farrow that the other prisoners were jealous of her beauty, and that her husband agreed to be bagged when meeting her for their sake. After that, Percy's attempt to find out which arm Farrow was missing by 'testing' his wife to ensure that she's not a 'gloater' seems positively inspired. Later, Percy suggests that Farrow's separated head and body could be taken to the Queen, as if he'd only just said something treacherous and been killed for it. Pathetic, contemptible and worth a try!

Cutting Comments: In fact, there are lots of comments about cutting, but that's by the by. 'To you, Baldrick,' says Blackadder, 'the Renaissance was just something that happened to other people, wasn't it?' He considers that Percy's huge new ruff makes him look like 'a bird who's swallowed a plate', and therefore sexy only in the eyes of 'another plate-swallowing bird . . . if it was blind and hadn't had it in months.' He also calls him a 'sad, laughable figure' and worries that, if they were to visit the Queen together, then people might get the impression that they're friends. When Percy cracks a feeble joke, Blackadder warns him never to attempt humour in his presence again, and, when Percy tells him that 'tiny' is fashionable, he remarks that he must have 'the most fashionable brain in London.' He has apparently never met anyone more repulsive than Gaoler Ploppy, and, upon hearing of the high jinks that he and Mistress Ploppy get up to, he comments drolly, 'The long winter evenings must fly by.' Explaining the part of his plan that involves obscuring Baldrick's features with a bag, he implies that this ought to be reason enough for him to wear it. Even while pretending to be Lord Farrow, he can't resist telling his 'little pumpkinny-wumpkinny' that persons unknown have been calling her 'a nosy little strumpet who's always going blubbing to the Queen.'

You Horrid Little Man: Blackadder has no qualms at all about doing the Queen's bidding, even when Percy attests to Farrow's innocence. He boasts that, beneath his 'boyish, playful exterior beats the heart of a ruthless, sadistic maniac'. When it looks like someone's for the chop, he has every intention of saving his own skin by sacrificing Percy.

Suspiciously Modern: Blackadder blames the death of the last Lord High Executioner on 'bloody red tape'. Gaoler Ploppy and cook Mistress Ploppy (no relation) would like to give the gaol a family atmosphere, which apparently means making it a place of pain, misery and sorrow. 'Mistress Ploppy's a bit of a social realist,' explains Ploppy.

Blackadder: The closing theme tells us: 'His great grandfather was a king, although for only thirty seconds.' Surprisingly, he tries to teach Baldrick the rudiments of addition, although his patience doesn't last the course. His main goal, when appointed Lord High Executioner, is to do as little work as possible. He comes on strong to Lady Farrow, but has nevertheless reached the age of thirty without anyone ever . . . er, doing what she tries to do to him. On her knees. With her mouth.

Baldrick: He hasn't mastered the concept of counting. In fact, he hasn't mastered the concept of thinking either, copying all his opinions from his master. He moonlights as an executioner – well, it's a hobby. He ensures that he cuts off the right bit by checking that it has a nose.

Percy: He would dearly love to be fashionable and sexy, but the huge ruff is a big mistake and so is the tiny one. As Blackadder's deputy, he is well prepared as usual, bringing along a soapbox on which he can stand to address the staff. Of course, they ignore him utterly.

Queenie: She has to be right about everything, to the point of forcing Melchett to admit that elephants are orange. She cuts off the heads of Catholics as a matter of course, but she's also executed some of her oldest friends (she's known Farrow since childhood). She's sure they won't have minded, it's just her little way. In fact, she deals death on a whim: she pardons

Farrow because 'he probably is innocent anyway', chats with her old friend Ponsonby a few days before she has him killed, and she sizes up Blackadder's head for a spike in Traitors' Cloister just out of curiosity. She's very keen on Blackadder, but you can see now why he's always so desperate to accommodate her changeable whims.

Melchett: He has a great deal of influence with the Queen, which he uses to make life difficult for Blackadder. He knows just how to keep that influence, too: when the Queen reiterates one of his suggestions, he congratulates her fawningly.

Nursie: She has a remedy for every ill: when the Queen's sister, Mary, had her head cut off, Nursie gave her some ointment and assured her it would soon grow back. She thinks she could stand up to the Queen if she wanted something particularly naughty, but the truth is that she just does as she's told. She doesn't seem to realise that discussing the odorous effects of the Queen's infant bowel movements in public just isn't on. She's also a bit too curious for her own good.

Name Checks: Blackadder's 'hit list' includes Admiral Lord Effingham, Sir Francis Drake, Buckingham and Ponsonby. The queen has already had Essex killed. Gaoler Ploppy, a sort of prototype Baldrick, is the son of Ploppy the Slopper.

The World According to Lord Blackadder: In a barbed attack on the Queen's policies, he describes himself as 'the new minister in charge of religious genocide'.

Essential Knowledge: Baldrick must have failed to kill Sir Francis Drake too, as he lived on until a bout of fever did for him at sea in 1596.

3: POTATO

First Broadcast: 23 January 1986.

Captain Rum (Tom Baker)
Sir Walter Raleigh (Simon Jones)

London celebrates the return of Sir Walter Raleigh – apart from Blackadder, that is. When Raleigh gains the Queen's favour, Blackadder rashly vows to outdo him by sailing the Sea of Certain Death. His captain will be the only man mad enough to take the job, the literally legless Redbeard Rum. The queen is impressed almost to the point of marriage – but Blackadder is actually planning to spend six months in the Dordogne. Good thing too, as Rum doesn't know where the Cape of Good Hope is. Trouble is, he doesn't know where France is either. The lost sailors are soon at the urine-drinking stage (though Rum started before the water ran out). Only Baldrick can provide, so it's lucky for all concerned that they suddenly hit land. Unfortunately, said land is infested by cannibalistic natives. Two years later, Blackadder, Percy and Baldrick return, Rum having sacrificed his life to save them. Thanks to Raleigh's interminable tales, though, the Queen is bored with explorers and interested only in presents. A boomerang keeps her amused – at least, once it proves its worth by knocking out Percy. And, for Melchett and Raleigh, there's a flask of suspiciously coloured wine.

Watch Out For: A good episode for fans of TV science fiction, with both the fourth *Doctor Who* and Arthur Dent from *The Hitch-Hikers' Guide to the Galaxy* starring.

Cunning Plans: Baldrick hides Percy in a box so that he can get out of being Blackadder's first mate. The plan isn't described as cunning, though, which is just as well because it isn't.

Cutting Comments: When Baldrick professes himself proud to be 'a member of the greatest kingdom on earth,' Blackadder has no doubts that 'many other members of the animal kingdom feel the same way.' He calls Raleigh a 'barnacle-bottomed, haddock-flavoured bilge rat'. 'Damned courtiers to the Queen,' says Captain Rum, 'you're nothing but lapdogs to a slip of a girl.' 'Better a lapdog to a slip of a girl,' Blackadder wittily ripostes, 'than a git!'

You Horrid Little Man: Blackadder kicks a door into Percy's face, then threatens to scoop out his head and turn it

into a novelty vase. He likens Baldrick's request for leave to
the actions of the fourteenth-century Peasants' Revolt leader,
Wat Tyler, and tells him he can take an afternoon off when he
dies. When a child taunts him by calling him 'sourpuss' and
'grumpy-face', he fires an arrow into the little cherub.

Double Entendres: It's a Tuesday, so Captain Rum can
probably be found 'up the Old Sea Dog'. As for the Old Sea
Dog, well, he'll be in bed with the captain. Obviously. Rum
wagers that Blackadder's purse has 'never had sixteen ship-
wrecked mariners tossing in it,' and, guess what, he's right.

Suspiciously Modern: The Queen warns Blackadder not to
eat foreign food. As Blackadder's crew panics, Rum's voice
cuts across the clamour with the words, 'Rhubarb, rhubarb,
rhubarb, rhubarb.'

Blackadder: We see him doing some actual work (of the paper
kind), though we don't know what. He tells Melchett that he
talks to himself to be sure of intelligent conversation. Determined not to welcome Raleigh at the palace, he is lured there
nonetheless by Melchett's casual remark that he's not very
popular with the Queen at the moment. He is easily provoked
into a rash promise when Raleigh humiliates him before the
Queen. He claims to 'laugh in the face of fear and tweak the
nose of terror', and he has a pragmatic response to Raleigh's
warning that the rain around the Cape of Good Hope will make
his head bleed: 'So, some sort of hat is probably in order.'
According to Rum, he has a woman's hands, a woman's skin,
a woman's purse, a woman's mouth and a woman's legs.

Baldrick: He plans to lie to Blackadder about the whereabouts
of the hidden Percy, but he can't quite manage it. Whether
that's through stupidity or fear of his master is unclear.

Percy: Given the unwanted position of first mate to Blackadder, he pretends to be bold but is forced to confess to
Baldrick that he's terrified of water, even if it's in a glass.
Apparently, the phobia stems from a savage turbot attack
during his youth. He spends the early stages of the voyage
sulking, and doesn't even join in the 'ha-haaaa's.

Queenie: She joins in the festivities by dressing up as a pirate and trying to play the part. She wants to look 'absolutely divine and regal' when Raleigh arrives, 'and yet at the same time very pretty and rather accessible.' She might even marry him, if he's gorgeous – and apparently he is, for she lets him sit on her throne while she admires his legs and points out the location of her bedroom at an inappropriate moment. She has some pretty wild dreams: once, she was sitting right on top of an enormous tree, and, on another occasion, she was a sausage roll. When Blackadder announces his ill-fated expedition, she remembers how dishy he is, and writes a poem called 'Edmund' for him ('When the sky is blue, And the cows go "moo"'). It's all a far cry from the days when, according to Nursie, she could only say 'Lizzie go plop-plop.' She gets all maternal towards Blackadder, to the point of checking that he has clean underwear; in his absence, she gets so bored with Raleigh that she orders him executed, but she lets him off when he blubs on his way to the block.

Melchett: He plays up appallingly to the Queen's pathetic pirate joke, prompting Blackadder to label him an 'utter creep'. Fair enough really, if a bit of a case of pots and kettles. Melchy also attempts a 'sea dog' act of his own, but can't quite lose his class and dignity, hence: 'with a yo-ho-ho and, perhaps I might venture, a bottle of rum into the bargain.'

Nursie: She throws herself at Rum upon learning that he likes enormous bottoms. She agrees to be the captain of his ship forever and is distraught at news of his death. Fortunately, Blackadder has salvaged his beard, which Nursie promises to wear forever in his memory.

Name Checks: Mrs Miggins from the pie shop misses the celebrations because she's bedridden from the nose down; even so, she makes a commemorative pie shaped, imaginatively, like an enormous pie. Shakespeare provides the title for Queenie's poem, 'Edmund'. When Percy goes to sea, he leaves behind his latest girlfriend, Lady Caroline Fairfax, whom Blackadder knows too.

The World According to Lord Blackadder: He resents the adulation accorded to 'bloody explorers', as opposed to 'the people who do all the work'. Baldrick suggests that 'the people who do all the work' are the servants, but Blackadder was thinking of himself. He is particularly jealous of the wealth and fame enjoyed by Raleigh after his discovery of the (to Blackadder, useless) potato. He doesn't want to meet him, as he fears he'll be subjected to 'three hours of bluff seaman's talk about picking the weevils out of biscuits and drinking urine'.

Essential Knowledge: History has rightly forgotten the strange circumstances that resulted in a horse becoming pope.

4: MONEY

First Broadcast: 6 February 1986.

Bishop of Bath and Wells (Ronald Lacey)
Mollie (Cassie Stuart)
Mrs Pants (Lesley Nicol)
Arthur the Sailor (John Pierce Jones)
Mad Beggar (Tony Aitken)
Leonardo Acropolis (Philip Pope)
Messenger (Piers Ibbotson)
Mr Pants (Barry Craine)

Blackadder is roused from his prostitute by a visit from the baby-eating Bishop of Bath and Wells. The bishop is assistant manager of the Bank of the Black Monks of St Herod, from whom Blackadder borrowed a thousand pounds one year ago. They want repayment or revenge. Faced with a choice between stumping up or dying in agony with a red-hot poker up his catflap, Blackadder opts for the former. But he doesn't have a thousand pounds, and his attempts to raise it are constantly interrupted by the Queen's practical jokes. Percy fails to discover the secrets of alchemy, and Baldrick's stint as a rent boy helps little, as a good hard shag from him is only worth sixpence. So, Blackadder sells his house, only to have the Queen filch the proceeds as another jape. Poker time approaches – until Blackadder has the bishop drugged and placed in a compromising position. Even the bish, sexual pervert though he is, is appalled at what he has been made to do. And England's finest portrait painter was on hand to capture the details. But who was the bishop's partner in these unspeakable acts? Who would plumb the depths of degradation just to save Blackadder's hide?

Watch Out For: Philip Pope was one of Tony Robinson's co-stars in the Channel 4 sketch show *Who Dares Wins*.

Cunning Plans: It's Baldrick who points out that Blackadder could make money at the docks doing favours for sailors – so, of course, it's Baldrick who ends up with the 'Get it Here' sign. He suggests gambling his hard-earned sixpence on a cock fight, preferably on a bird with odds of 40,000 to 1 – perhaps a killer bull that's been disguised as a bird by having feathers stuck to it and an egg hung between its legs. Percy 'cunningly' fashions jewellery from purest 'green', in the hope of selling it for profit. In the end, Blackadder has to get himself out of trouble, with a plan 'so cunning you could brush your teeth with it.'

Cutting Comments: Blackadder has a fine line in sarcasm when the Queen tries his patience. 'Thank God I wore my corset, because I think my sides have split.' 'I only didn't laugh out loud because I was afraid, if I did, my head would have fallen off.' ('If you don't start soon,' says the Queen, 'your head *will* fall off.') When Percy makes the mistake of hugging him, he says, 'I was just thinking, "My God, I die in twelve hours, what I really need now is a hug from a complete prat."' Displaying his painting to the bishop, he remarks, 'I think you probably recognise this huge, sweating mound of blubber here.'

You Horrid Little Man: Blackadder pushes a poor, mad beggar into a water-filled ditch. He found Percy's savings some time ago, stole them and spent them. And the same goes for the two farthings Baldrick hid inside a mouldy potato. Mr Pants agrees to pay him a thousand pounds for his house, but he has Baldrick beat him up (literally) to eleven hundred.

Double Entendres: Blackadder introduces Mollie as a dear friend, but in fact she's quite inexpensive. 'What's that in your tights?' the Queen demands of Blackadder, pointing out a suspicious bulge. As it turns out, it's just over a thousand pounds.

Suspiciously Modern: The Bank of the Black Monks has branches everywhere. The Bishop admits that he'll do anything to anything, on which Blackadder comments, 'Nice to hear the Church speaking out for a change on social issues.' And, of course, there's the whole Elizabethan slant on the incriminating photo – 'Anyway, we have the preliminary sketches.'

Blackadder: He pays for a prostitute, and wants to do things so horrible that they're worth an extra sixpence. He's always lying to the Queen about how wealthy he is, in order to improve his standing at Court. In fact, he boasts that he's 'one of England's finest fibsters'. He has only eighty-five pounds in the world – until the Queen takes it off him. His father blew the family fortune on wine, women and amateur dramatics, and had to eke out a living 'doing humorous impressions of Anne of Cleves.' He lives in Billingsgate. He uses his charm only where it will do the most good – so he turns it on for potential house-buyer Timothy Pants, but not for his critical wife. When Pants accuses him of having his banter prepared, Blackadder replies, 'This is a different thing: it's spontaneous and it's called wit.' His house provides 'the very latest in front-wall fresh-air orifices combined with a wide-capacity gutter installation below,' i.e., he craps out of the window. He is surprised and annoyed to learn that people call him 'Old Privy Breath' and liken him to dogs' business. The Bishop, self-confessed colossal pervert though he is, tells Blackadder he's never encountered 'such corrupt and foul-minded perversity', and asks if he's considered a career in the Church.

Baldrick: He eats dung. On Blackadder's say-so, he beats up Mr Pants to get money out of him (he may have done the same thing to Kate's father in 'Bells').

Percy: He is shocked to hear that Blackadder fibs to the Queen, and gullible enough to believe that a giant humming-bird has pounced on his outer garments when Blackadder demonstrates his lying skills. Everyone knows where he keeps – or rather kept – his savings. He is hopelessly opti-mistic, believing that an hour's ceaseless searching will reveal to him the secret of alchemy. As it is, he manages to turn base things into 'green', which comes not in nuggets but in splats. For the first time, it's made clear that he lives with Blackadder rather than being a frequent guest, though he has no financial stake in the house. His full name is Lord Percy Percy and he is heir to the Duchy of Northumberland. He's extremely loyal to Blackadder, despite all the abuse he receives from him – and, of course, he's willing to plumb the depths of degradation just to save his hide.

Queenie: She has a bet with Melchett that Blackadder will fall for her practical jokes, 'because I'm so super and you're so stupid.' She occupies herself by playing games of chess and shove-halfpenny with Melchett and Nursie.

Melchett: He claims to be broke. Despite encouraging the Queen's japes, he isn't pleased to have the tables turned. When the Queen pretends that she's about to have him exe-cuted for 'taking the mickey out of my beloved Edmund so cruelly', he bursts into tears.

Name Checks: William Greaves, another Black Monk cus-tomer, was born in Chelmsford in 1513 and died fifty years later with a spike up his bottom. Cardinal Wolsey once got his knob out at Hampton Court and pretended to be a door. A slap-up binge at Mrs Miggins's Pie Shop costs only thruppence.

Essential Knowledge: It's in the closing theme: 'Take heed the moral of this tale, Be not a borrower or lender, And if your finances do fail, Make sure your banker's not a bender.'

5: BEER

First Broadcast: 13 February 1986.

Lady Whiteadder (Miriam Margolyes)
Simon Partridge (Hugh Laurie)
Geoffrey Piddle (Roger Blake)
Monk (William Hootkins)
Lord Whiteadder (Daniel Thorndike)

Blackadder's rich but puritanical aunt and uncle, Lord and
Lady Whiteadder, invite themselves to dinner to discuss his
inheritance. But the Queen manoeuvres Blackadder and
Melchett into a drinking competition with ten thousand
florins at stake. Trying to keep a debauched piss-up and a
refined family meal of Baldrick's turnip surprise separate,
Blackadder makes mistakes. He gets away with the thingy-
shaped turnip and the comedy breasts – and, even when a
drunken friar congratulates him on a 'great booze-up', he's
able to pass it off as a reference to Great Boo, the tribal chief
who has just recovered from a sleeping sickness. But when a
curious queen turns up in disguise, Blackadder locks her in a
cupboard – and his plan to drink water instead of ale is rum-
bled. Melchett forces him to down a flagon, and, forty-two
seconds later, a cardinal's hat and an ostrich feather in his
britches give away his inebriated state. Nor does his use of
the word 'fart' help. The inheritance is lost and Lord
Whiteadder inadvertently releases the Queen. The revellers
mistake her for a stripper, and it looks like heads will roll.
But first, the Queen decides to have a little drinky.

Cutting Comments: 'It is said, Percy, that civilised man
seeks out good and intelligent company so that, through
learned discourse, he may rise above the savage and closer to
God . . . Personally, however, I like to start the day with a
total dickhead to remind me I'm best.' That's from Blackadder, of course. He also tells Baldrick that his breath comes
'straight from Satan's bottom'. When the Queen mistakes

Melchett's hangover for a life-threatening illness and insists that something ought to be done, Blackadder answers, 'Yes, of course. Some sort of celebration.'

You Horrid Little Man: Blackadder wants to write out party invitations in blood. Baldrick's blood, to be precise. Believing the disguised Queen to be Percy's girlfriend, he locks her in a cupboard. When Percy accidentally brings up the subject of brothels in front of the Whiteadders, Blackadder kicks him so hard that he falls off his chair. There's a repeat performance when Percy draws attention to a drunken roar from across the hall.

Double Entendres: Plenty of them. The Queen is wakened by a 'terrific banging from Lord Melchett' – on the castle gates, of course. When Blackadder wants Baldrick's blood, Baldrick wonders if he should cut off an arm or a leg. 'A little prick should do,' is his master's response. 'When you call for ale,' says Baldrick, trying to get to grips with Blackadder's plan, 'I pass water.' Party guest Simon Partridge sees double entendres everywhere; even the word 'tick' sounds a bit like . . . er, 'bum'. When Lady Whiteadder catches Blackadder wearing a pair of 'devil's dumplings', he shifts them to his head with the exclamation: 'Oh my God, my earmuffs have fallen down!' The Queen gets a bit tipsy and forgets her promise to execute everyone. 'I'm sure there was something very important I had to do to all of you this morning.' But all of this pales to insignificance next to the turnip that's exactly the same shape as a thingy, particularly when Lady Whiteadder gets stuck into it. It reminds her of her wedding night, apparently (she ate raw turnip then, too).

Suspiciously Modern: Blackadder criticises Percy for using the phrase 'beshrew me'.

Tortuous Similes: When Melchett accuses Blackadder of twisting and turning 'like a twisty-turny thing', he starts off a trend . . .

Blackadder: His family has been plagued with syphilis for three decades. He's famous for not being able to take his beer: when the King of Austria visited, he was found wandering around Hampton Court, naked, singing 'I'm Merlin, the Happy Pig' – and, last time he got drunk, the Queen found him 'face down in a puddle, wearing a pointy hat and singing a song about goblins'. Apparently, the goblin song turns up whenever he's had one drop of the ale. He's suspiciously defensive on the subject of thingy size.

Baldrick: He takes to lying on the floor with cheese hanging from his nose in the hope that a mouse might scurry into his mouth – until he gets fed up with an all-mouse diet and hangs a mouse from his nose in order to catch a cat. Charged with preparing a meal for vegetarians, he offers up his turnip surprise. He's been in Blackadder's family since 1532 (according to 'Bells', he joined it when he was two and a half, so, if we accept the pre-publicity dating of this episode as 1565, he must now be thirty-five or thirty-six). As Blackadder's bondsman, he's prepared to obey his every word, even if it means cutting off his 'little prick' – which, ironically, is the same shape as a turnip. Sometimes, he hides in vegetable racks at parties and frightens the children.

Percy: He would love to be an actor; he dabbled a little in his youth, and considered himself to be the man of a thousand faces. He thinks he knows how to handle a woman, though sweet-talking Lady Whiteadder is a big mistake. He asks Lord Whiteadder to tell him all about his vow of silence.

Queenie: She loves it when Blackadder gets cross and sometimes thinks about having him executed just to see the expression on his face. 'I may have the body of a weak and feeble woman,' she proclaims, 'but I have the heart and stomach of a concrete elephant.' She's willing to prove it, too.

Melchett: His annual communion wine-tasting is a no-holds-barred event, with curried turtle laid on. His golden comedy breasts are larger and more ornate than anybody else's.

Nursie: Her cure for a hangover is to rub the tummy and entreat it to get better. She thinks that, if people have too many clever ideas, their feet fall off. After all, it happened to her brother, when he had the brilliant idea of cutting his toe-nails with a scythe. She is quite happy to treat Blackadder as one of her charges and insists that he has his bath. She's also under the impression that grown men wear nappies.

Name Checks: Cardinal Wolsey is 'an aggressive drunken lout with the intelligence of a four-year-old and the sexual sophistication of a donkey,' making him a prime candidate for a party invitation. Percy has yet another girlfriend: Gwendolyn. Dr McGlue's Amber Enema is one of the most potent beers known to man.

The World According to Lady Whiteadder: She and her husband sit on a single spike at home, and may only suffer the comfort of Blackadder's chairs if they can stick forks in their legs between courses. She eats no meat and sees the mashing of turnips as the work of Beelzebub, 'for Satan saw God's blessed turnip and he envied it and mashed it to spoil its sacred shape.' She doesn't like the presence of other people, as it offers the possibility of fornication. She thinks that 'cold is God's way of telling us to burn more Catholics.' She hates references to family, as they provide evidence of sex. She doesn't know that Nathaniel's vow of silence only applies when she's listening. But then, under threat of execution, she gets drunk like everyone else, after which she can't help noticing that the word 'luck' sounds almost exactly like 'fuck'.

Essential Knowledge: The surprise is that there's nothing in it except the turnip.

6: CHAINS

First Broadcast: 20 February 1986.

> Prince Ludwig (Hugh Laurie)
> Torturer (Max Harvey)
> 1st Guard (Mark Arden)
> 2nd Guard (Lee Cornes)

The Queen agrees to pay a ransom demand, but it must be the last one ever. Which is unfortunate for Blackadder, as he's just been kidnapped. And Melchett's next. Facing torture, Blackadder is quite prepared to talk. Now, if only his captor could speak English. He's about to have his testicles removed with a blunt garden instrument – though he can't quite work out what – when the evil German plotter and master of disguise Prince Ludwig reveals himself. He makes his demands, and the Queen has to choose whom to save. Unable to decide, she lashes out the cash on a fancy dress party instead, unaware that Ludwig plots to depose her and become master of the world. Blackadder and Melchett buy their lives with information, then escape and return to the palace while the party is in progress. Blackadder runs his sword through the very realistic cow that's sitting in Nursie's place – which is where Ludwig made his mistake, of course. As a master of disguise, his cow costume was much better than anything that Nursie could ever manage. Unfortunately, Ludwig slaughters the entire court and uses his disguise skills to take the Queen's place.

Watch Out For: Mark Arden also played a guard in 'Witchsmeller Pursuivant'. He and Lee Cornes were stalwarts of the famous Comedy Store in its early days.

Cunning Plans: Blackadder watches the guards' routine and selects the moment when they're at their most vulnerable. The cunning bit is that, during the 'insulting farewell gestures to the prisoners', he and Melchett punch them where it will do the most good, then flee. The only drawback is that Blackadder gets the hard one.

Cutting Comments: Baldrick mentions that he's recently heard an amusing story, to which Blackadder replies, 'Oh, good!' before walking off. The torturer calls Blackadder a 'bastard son of a bitch', but the insult loses some of its potency through being mimed. Blackadder launches into a diatribe against Ludwig, who is apparently 'essential at all social gatherings: the tedious little turd who keeps putting on amusing voices.' Although he quite likes the 'fat-headed

German chamber pot' voice that Ludwig does all the time. Melchett suggests passing time with a pleasant word game, so Blackadder starts by challenging him to construct a sentence from the words 'face', 'sodding', 'your' and 'shut'. To Percy's delight, Blackadder claims to have missed him. Indeed, throughout his captivity, he often thought: 'I wish Percy was here – being tortured instead of me.'

You Horrid Little Man: Blackadder once told his aunt to get stuffed when she asked him for money to ransom her husband. He drags Melchett down a flight of stairs to ensure that he can escape first. He makes two attempts to kill Ludwig, with a sword and a dagger. And he catches up to that balladeer at last, and dunks him in a fountain repeatedly.

Double Entendres: 'As private parts to the gods we are,' moans Melchett. 'They play with us for their sport.'

Suspiciously Modern: Prince Ludwig refers to 'naughty parchments', obviously a forerunner of naughty magazines; amongst his repertoire of silly voices, Blackadder suggests, is a 'side-splitting poof'. He was bullied at school and forced by his mother to wear shorts right up to his final year.

Blackadder: He appears to be finally living up to his ancestor's reputation by ordering Melchett and the Queen out of the throne room. But he's just telling them the story of how he was caught with his tights down with a 'whore slut painted strumpet', presumably by said strumpet's husband. He escaped through the privy window. His most pressing worry, upon being kidnapped, is the embarrassment of it. He agrees to talk before any actual torture takes place, and he's perfectly willing to betray the Queen to save his life. He used to 'dine and plot and play the biscuit game' with Otto, a black marketeer and smuggler, at the Old Pizzle in Dover. He slept with the Old Pizzle's waitress, Big Sally, unaware that she was Ludwig in a cunning disguise. He was paralytic at the time, and therefore a disappointment. Ludwig suggests that Blackadder finds himself amusing, to which he responds, 'I try not to fly in the face of public opinion.' He is unimpressed by Ludwig's posturing and quick to unearth its causes by psychoanalysis, with devastating accuracy. The sheep incident gives him something on Melchett at last, and he's not slow to use it.

Baldrick: He sticks a pencil up each nostril and goes to the party as a pencil case.

Percy: No one has ever solved the perplexing mystery of his Uncle Bertram, who disappeared along with his house, his old oak table and everything else he owned on the night of the great Stepney fire. Blackadder's insults seem to have made an impression, as Percy now thinks of himself as an idiot. He's unemployed.

Queenie: She plays frisbee with Percy, but insists that he let her win. As a baby, she preferred Nursie's milk to cow's milk, and wanted it from both breasty dumplings. She describes Blackadder and Melchett as her 'two faves' and can't choose between them. She dresses as her father for the party, but when Percy comments that it's like Henry VIII has been reborn, she says, 'Let's bally well hope not, or else I won't be queen any more.' When she was tiny, she had parties with tea and cakes and venison, after which she would take some of her little friends on a trip to the executions – that's if she wanted any of her little friends executed. She misses Blackadder because 'he always loved parties and always, always wore very very tight tights.' Her father used to take her riding on a magnificent grey pony, which she used to fondle and kiss. Prince Ludwig was the stable lad, although Queenie knew him as Shorty Greasy Spot Spot.

Melchett: He has an old tutor who is either Lord Forrest or Lord Forrest's son (it's not clear which). He goes to pieces at the thought of being hurt. He once stayed at a monastery in Cornwall, where he talked to an old shepherd called Timpkins and became intimate with Flossie, one of his sheep. But Flossie was Ludwig in a cunning disguise . . . Melchett is only slightly less willing than Blackadder to betray the Queen to save his life. His official title is presumably Lord Chamberlain, as Percy becomes Acting Lord Chamberlain in his absence.

Nursie: She enjoys the chance to pet Baldrick and feed him scraps (until the Queen later takes over). She breastfed the Queen. Despite suggesting that everyone should turn up to the party naked, she loves to dress up, so long as it's as 'a lovely, lovely cow with great big lovely udders.' In short, she's 'a sad, insane old woman with an udder fixation.'

Name Checks: Previous kidnapping victims include Lord Forrest's son and Blackadder's Uncle Osric.

The World According to Lord Blackadder: He asserts that anyone stupid enough to get kidnapped by some 'moustachioed dago' deserves everything they get.

Essential Knowledge: It's a scythe.

4: BLACKADDER THE THIRD

Hard Times

For the third set of instalments chronicling the saga of the notorious Blackadder family, TV biographers Richard Curtis and Ben Elton opened the annals during the reign of King George III, to examine the period in history known to many scholars as 1760–1815 (in publicity material for the series) or 1760–1827 (in the opening titles). This was a time of great upheaval, which saw revolutions in America and France. Britain, you'll recall (though only if you're several hundred years old), decided to keep its unelected monarch and opted for an industrial revolution instead.

The maintenance of the status quo is fortunate for the contemporaneous Mr Edmund Blackadder who, after a dip in the family fortunes, is forced to take employment as a butler in the royal household, and supplement his income by fleecing the Prince Regent. It is, in fact, quite a cushy number all round, allowing Blackadder the freedom to dabble in politics, writing and highway robbery. The only negative aspect of the job is the derision he is forced to endure from his peers for being the butler with the stupidest master.

The Blackadder Chronicles

To promote the 1987 series, *Radio Times* had producer John Lloyd tell 'Blackadder – the Untold Story', in which he revealed the existence of an ancient set of journals known as the Blackadder Chronicles, from which the television scripts were allegedly adapted. With the Blackadders expanding into a whole dynasty, the Chronicles provide a logical expansion of the hitherto untitled document that had supposedly been the source of information for events depicted in the first series.

At best, however, the Blackadder Chronicles must be regarded as an apocryphal work – or, as Lloyd described the documents, 'long, dull, and utter tosh from beginning to end'. For, as we know, it wasn't until the fifteenth century that the Blackadder dynasty was established (when, stealing an idea from Baldrick, Prince Edmund, Duke of Edinburgh decided to dub himself with that dark epithet for effect) – and yet the Chronicles make reference to Blackadders from as early as the tenth century. This is, of course, only possible if Donald, Third Duke of Argyll just so coincidentally happened to be Donald Blackadder.

One such unlikely antecedent is the Baron de Blackadder (1187–1217) who, because he couldn't see the point in it, didn't bother to sign the Magna Carta, thereby setting the standard for many subsequent Blackadders who missed out on history's great events. His descendant, who missed out on the Crusades, was so determined to play his part in the capture of the Holy Land that he led the failed twenty-third Crusade over August Bank Holiday Weekend 1972.

Less recently, Edmund T Blackadder was, as part of the Manhattan Project, assigned the important task of helping to bring the Second World War to a noisy conclusion; he eventually succeeded in helping to discover those little holes in the sides of biros. It seems that the Blackadder Chronicles delineate the family history right up to the present day; or at least until 1968 and a dinner party in Chelsea, at which Edmund Blackadder became the first man to deride flares. Artist Graham Higgins provided a nice little illustration of him and a duffle-coated Baldrick at this significant moment in British history, and it has to be said that anyone with a beard as ridiculous as the sixties Blackadder's is hardly qualified to make judgements on fashion, however crap.

Giving his opinion of the manuscripts, John Lloyd condemns them as 'a catalogue of breathtaking exaggerations, thunderous libels and outrageous lies' (they would even prove to be self-contradictory, as we'll learn in Chapter 7). The events that unfold in *Blackadder the Third* are adapted from the breathtaking exaggerations, thunderous libels and outrageous lies contained in Volume XIV.

Dramatis Personae

Few discernible character traits passed down the generations from the slimy gurning original Black Adder to his quasi-dashing Elizabethan descendant (well, apart from being quite bad, of course) – but, by the concluding bit of the eighteenth century, subtler changes to the family attributes are apparent. Despite his reduced circumstances, the Mr Edmund Blackadder who serves Prince George is perhaps the most deviously intelligent of them all. He is clean-shaven too, but there is good reason for that: 'My girlfriend hated that beard,' Rowan Atkinson told the *Radio Times* during the run of the third series. The change in the family status adds a little more rationale to Blackadder's scheming – and, though he would even stoop to murder if it aided his ambitions, thanks to Atkinson's expert portrayal, you can't help but like him.

Mr Blackadder is accompanied, of course, by Baldrick, his dogsbody: a walking dung heap with an interest in turnips that borders on obsession. Once again, an expansion in the Blackadder intellect is matched by a reduction in Baldrick's. Fortunately, this loss of brain power halts just before the Baldricks attain the same intellectual capacity as their beloved turnips, levelling off at seriously stupid.

Blackadder II had ended with Hugh Laurie's Germanic royal character Prince Ludwig substituting himself for Queen Elizabeth I and thus taking the throne of England – which was a good trick. Appropriately enough, this series has Laurie complete the threesome of central characters by playing another royal of German descent: the exceptionally dim-witted Prince George. Looking back at the series years later, *Sunday Times Magazine* reporter Matthew Gwyther described Laurie's performance as the Prince Regent as 'one of the greatest post-war creations on British television. As a study of gormlessness it has no equal.' Indeed, George is possibly even more stupid than Baldrick. He would be lost without his manservant, incapable even of putting on his own trousers without Mr Blackadder's help. He is also despised by both the establishment and the public at large, but too thick-skinned to realise.

Completing an unusually small line-up of recurring characters – and in little more than an extended cameo capacity at that – is Helen Atkinson-Wood (no relation to Rowan Atkinson) as Mrs Miggins, a name that was already familiar to *Blackadder* viewers. Despite appearing only in *Blackadder the Third*, the pie/coffee/horse's willy shop proprietor has become an integral part of *Blackadder* mythology; this is due in no small part to Atkinson-Wood's richly comic performance. No doubt the extent of this talent was first discovered when she attended Oxford and took part in the Atkinson and Curtis revues *Celebration* and *Beyond a Joke*. Over the years, she has been the female component that completed a couple of comedy teams, firstly joining Chris Tarrant, Lenny Henry and John Gorman in *OTT* (Over the Top), then becoming part of the award-winning *Radio Active/KYTV* team. Her television credits read like the index of an encyclopaedia of comedy, only with some programmes left out: *Alas Smith and Jones*, *Barbara*, *The Comic Strip*, *Girls on Top*, *Happy Families*, *Who Dares Wins* and *The Young Ones*, to name but a lot.

Blackadder the Third may have had a smaller regular cast than usual, but it certainly made up for it with its higher-than-usual count of guest stars. The Regency period was an age teeming with historical personalities deemed worthy of the full *Blackadder* treatment.

They Seek Him Here

Missing from Blackadder's circle of friends this time around is the imbecilic Lord Percy Percy. After being offered a number of other imbecilic roles, Tim McInnerny felt he was in danger of becoming typecast, and declined the opportunity to appear as Percy's Regency descendant (perhaps we can assume the line died out, given Percy's terrible record with female companions in *Blackadder II*). It's fortunate that Tony Robinson wasn't likewise perturbed about becoming too associated with a dullard, as the departure of Percy from the equation served to cement the Blackadder and Baldrick double act. Since then, as with other great pairings such as Laurel and Hardy, Morecambe and Wise or Lea and Perrins, it has become impossible to think of one without the other.

McInnerny does turn up, however, in the third episode of the series, 'Nob and Nobility', as none other than the Scarlet Pimpernel. While they frequently reinvented authentic historical luminaries when the storyline called for it, the *Blackadder* team rarely borrowed other writers' fictional creations. But, in this instance, Baroness Orczy's upper-crust English saviour of those upper-crust French selected for a date with Mme Guillotine provides more than just inspiration for the Revolutionary episode.

Not that Orczy's hero is copied wholesale. In the *Blackadder* version of the tale, the Pimpernel's true identity is revealed to be the foppish Lord Topper, instead of the foppish Sir Percy Blakeney as in the original series of novels. Well, having McInnerny play another Percy would just have been ironic, wouldn't it? Despite this alteration, extant copyright on the Scarlet Pimpernel – the swashbuckling character who inspired both Zorro and the Black Fingernail in *Carry On Don't Lose Your Head* – has precluded the broadcast of 'Nob and Nobility' on American television.

The inclusion of the Scarlet Pimpernel is just one example of literary influence in *Blackadder the Third*, the most blatantly bookish of the four series. This is noticeable right from the opening credits in which Blackadder peruses volumes such as *Encyclopaedia Blackaddica*, *Old Blackamoore's Almanac*, *Landscape Gardening* by Capability Brownadder, *The Blackobite Rebellion*, *From Black Death to Blackadder*, *Blackadder's Bedside Cockfighting Companion*, *Blackadder's Book of Martyrs*, etc. Most, if not all of these tomes have echoes of the fake history/Blackadder Chronicles thinking behind the series. And, though the books he eventually finds to represent the episodes may look a bit lurid (with their covers adorned by big-bosomed women), a hint of that well-known writer Jane Austen can be detected in the alliterative titles.

The erudite themes feature prominently in 'Ink and

Incapability', where Dr Johnson's dictionary provides the basis for the storyline, the Romantic poets Byron, Shelley and Coleridge put in a drug-addled appearance, and even Blackadder himself has literary aspirations under the guise of Gertrude Perkins.

The theatre and Shakespeare are revisited in 'Sense and Senility', and there's a touch of *Cyrano de Bergerac* about 'Amy and Amiability'. This episode sees a welcome guest appearance by Miranda Richardson who, like Tim McInnerny, plays a character with more than one personality; one who at first seems to be as vapid as her earlier creation, but who turns out to have an infinitely less vapid alter-ego. The roots of Richardson's character, the elusive Shadow, lie in the Gainsborough movie *The Wicked Lady*, in which Margaret Lockwood played a notorious highwayperson (much of the notoriety resulting from her expansive cleavage) – although, if memory serves, Miss Lockwood didn't have a problem with squirrels. The Shadow's disguised voice sounding, as it does, like James Mason further alludes to that film, because he was in it, too. Minus the mask, Richardson displays her versatility as a character actress as saccharin-sweet, vomit-inducing Amy Hardwood.

The inclusion of the Duke of Wellington in 'Duel and Duality' enables another *Blackadder II* regular, Stephen Fry, to put in a single appearance; the cannon-toting 'Iron Duke' is light years away from the refined Lord Melchett of the previous series, although he would prove to be a template for Fry's character in the next one. The role of the thunderous and angry Wellington presented Fry with the opportunity to hit Hugh Laurie at regular intervals. Several years later, in an on-line chat with the AOL *Black Adder* club, he made amends by complimenting his comedy partner's performance thus: 'People don't realise often that the skill in screen violence comes from the receiver, not the puncher.'

Regency Ramblings

With its immediate predecessor having made such good use of a small number of sets, there was to be no return to the great outdoors for *Blackadder the Third*. It was, however, granted the luxury of three regular sets: Prince George's chambers (with attached vestibule) and the kitchen were supplemented by Mrs Miggins's Coffee Shoppe, the social heart of Regency London. The studio-bound set-up in itself occasionally worked to the writers' advantage, allowing them to get in mocking jibes at the expense of the programme's limited environs: the unrealistic grassy knoll in 'Amy and Amiability', for instance. The obviously painted bit of scenery that provided the backdrop to the series' climactic duel was a little too unrealistic, however.

Blackadder II had hit upon a winning formula, to which few changes were made this time around. Although Baldrick's cunning plans had been a mainstay since day one, they grew even more preposterous in this series, and their elevated status made them a much anticipated feature of each new episode. Blackadder also gained his own belated trademark, in the form of those absurd similes that we now associate so closely with the character. After a brief appearance in Melchett's dialogue in the *Blackadder II* episode 'Beer', these tortuous constructions began to crop up in the episodes as frequently as something very frequent indeed – and they weren't limited exclusively to Edmund's dialogue. Stephen Fry was especially fond of them, as he recalled on-line: 'It was wonderful really. The main trouble was that the scripts were changed all the time until the last moment. John Lloyd, Hugh and I in particular would rewrite until the final moments, we endlessly had "epithet moments" as we called them . . . Sticky the stick insect, that kind of thing, asthmatic ants with particularly heavy shopping, all those sorts of jokes. Somehow there was never enough time to get them absolutely right. We used to wriggle about screaming with adolescent laughter whenever we did those. But some work much better than others.'

You can judge for yourself, as we now include Tortuous Similes in our episode write-ups.

In a contrast to the previous two series, no specific dates are given to set the scene for individual episodes of *Blackadder the Third* – perhaps because of bloody great anachronisms such as Dr Johnson hanging out with junkie poets Byron and Shelley, when by rights they shouldn't have been born until after Johnson's death. Doubtless there are other examples of historical inconsistencies to be found, but it would require someone who gave a toss to search them out.

One event that certainly didn't happen in real life, though, is the death of the Prince Regent at the hands of the Duke of Wellington, as detailed in the final episode, 'Duel and Duality'. Even so, this hardly came as a shock to long-time *Blackadder* viewers who, by this time, were conditioned to expect fatalities among the regular cast. What *is* an unexpected turn, however, is that Edmund Blackadder survives the series and, what's more, assumes George's identity. What this means, of course, is that a member of the dynasty almost certainly sat on the throne of England under the guise of King George IV. Again, if you want to know what became of King Blackadder after the series ended, read a history book or something. However, the fact that George IV didn't die until 1830, some three years after the date given on screen for the end of Blackadder's life, suggests that the full story hasn't been told yet.

Reactions

Although it was merely an attempt to recreate the style of a Regency playbill, the end credits' description of *Blackadder the Third* as 'Mr Curtis and Mr Elton's Much admir'd comedy' might have been slightly embarrassing if it hadn't in fact been much admired. As it happened, though, it was admired enough to garner a BAFTA award for Best Light Entertainment Series. But did the hard-to-please press critics admire it?

'Rowan Atkinson's timing was as killingly perfect as ever,' said Hilary Kingsley in the *Daily Mirror*; her comment was fairly typical of the reviews and, on the whole, *Blackadder the Third* received a better reception than its predecessors. Some critics still managed to find fault, however.

Reviewing the first episode, the *Mail*'s Philip Purser suspected that 'Richard Curtis and Ben Elton's sturdy schoolboy

humour and Rowan Atkinson's sinister application of it were
better suited to the medieval goings-on of the previous series.
It was significant that they lapsed into a spot of roasting poor
Baldrick on a spit that was quite out of fashion by 1804.'

Ian Curtis of the *Express* was almost won over: 'Funny?
Yes, but I can't say I found this show an unmitigated delight.
Baldrick's preoccupation with turnips was just silly. And I
was just as numb about the matter of the Prince's socks that
were obviously being stolen by Blackadder for private profit.
Still the timing of the main characters was impeccable, and
there were enough good gags to make me look forward to
next week's episode.'

Writing in her Saturday TV column, the *Express*'s other
reviewer, the frequently vitriolic Nina Myskow, was unam-
bivalent in her opinion. She claimed to love *Blackadder*
'despite being hopeless at sums.' It took us ages to work out
that one.

Blackadder the Third

Edmund Blackadder, butler to the Prince
(Mr Rowan Atkinson)
Baldrick, a dogsbody (Mr Tony Robinson)
Prince George, the Prince Regent, their master
(Mr Hugh Laurie)
Mrs Miggins, a coffee shoppekeeper
(Miss Helen Atkinson-Wood)

Written by Richard Curtis and Ben Elton; directed by
Mandie Fletcher; produced by John Lloyd.

1: DISH AND DISHONESTY

First Broadcast: 17 September 1987.

Mr Vincent Hanna, his own great-great-great-grandfather
(Mr Vincent Hanna)
Sir Talbot Buxomly, a Member of Parliament (Mr Denis Lill)
Pitt the Younger, the Prime Minister (Mr Simon Osborne)
Pitt the Even Younger, a tiny Whig
(Master Dominic Martelli)
Ivor Biggun, a candidate (Mr Geoff McGivern)

Due to his excessive spending on socks, George will be
stricken from the Civil List if new Prime Minister Pitt the
Younger has his way. But in the Commons, opinion is evenly
divided and Blackadder, eager to remain in his first-class

carriage on the gravy train, hopes to tip the balance in the Prince's favour with Sir Talbot Buxomly's deciding vote. Buxomly's sudden death rather thwarts that plan. Instead Blackadder decides to fill the vacancy in Buxomly's former constituency Dunny-on-the-Wold with an MP totally under his control. Enter Baldrick, a rotten candidate for a rotten borough. With Blackadder himself installed as the only eligible voter, Baldrick wins by a landslide, which proves rather upsetting for Pitt the Even Younger, standing at his brother's behest. Baldrick, of course, votes the wrong way and the Prince is abolished. But all is not lost, there's still the House of Lords . . . Just to be on the safe side, Blackadder suggests to George that he bribes the existing lords and makes a new one of, mentioning no names, someone in his employ who has been steadfast against Pitt's machinations. Enter Lord Baldrick and exit the bribery money, spent on a vast turnip.

Watch Out For: *Only Fools and Horses* star Denis Lill in padding as the ill-fated Sir Talbot Buxomly who, before he died, enjoyed flogging servants and shooting poor people, and who favoured extending slavery to include anyone without a knighthood.

Cunning Plans: Blackadder's idea to purchase Dunny-in-the-Wold in the Suffolk fens and control its voter is sound, as is his decision to install a puppet MP. The only real flaw in the plan is his choice of representative.

Cutting Comments: George is oblivious to the fact that he's being insulted when Sir Talbot says he's 'the son of a certified sauerkraut-sucking loon' with the dress sense of a mad parrot, who talks like 'a plate of beans negotiating their way out of a cow's digestive system' and is thus a less able Regent than a piece of lemon peel. Blackadder is quick to agree when Mrs Miggins claims to have the brains of a sultana.

You Horrid Little Man: Not that there's any proof of Blackadder's involvement, mind you, but it was a bit suspicious that the previous Dunny-on-the-Wold voter accidentally cut his head off while combing his hair, allowing Blackadder to step in and take his place. Just as it was slightly suspect that the returning officer brutally stabbed himself in the stomach while shaving, again allowing Blackadder to step in. When his political efforts come to nothing, he repays Baldrick by roasting him on a spit.

Double Entendres: While unintentionally patronising Pitt the Younger, George assumes the youthful Prime Minister is on half hols and can't wait to get a bat in his hands and give some balls a good walloping. Blackadder's £1000 'leather-trimmed ermine gown with gold medallion accessories' turns out to be made of real cats, including one that belonged to a certain Emma Hamilton – so, now he can go to fancy dress parties as Lady Hamilton's pussy.

Suspiciously Modern: Along with fraudulent and sexually deviant MPs, the announcing of the election results does not appear to have changed much over the centuries. They weren't broadcast on the telly or anything back then, that would be silly, but an ancestor of the late *Newsnight* reporter Vincent Hanna was on hand to describe the proceedings. Ivor 'Jest Ye Not Madame' Biggun's Standing at the Back Dressed Stupidly and Looking Stupid Party could almost be a forerunner of the Monster Raving Loony Party, only without the modern equivalent's sensible policies.

Tortuous Similes: As a Prime Minister, Blackadder feels that Pitt the Elder was 'about as effective as a cat flap in an elephant house'.

Blackadder: He is, according to the PM, a lower-middle-class yobbo. As well as working as a butler in the royal household, he has a lucrative sideline selling the Prince's socks via a Tunisian hosiery merchant. He forms the Adder Party, but has no real political ambitions: he just wants to continue making money out of the Prince. He almost regains the family title, which has somehow been mislaid over the years. If only his hints to George were less subtle.

Baldrick: His sole aim in life is the acquisition of turnips – though what he wants them for is unclear, as he eats dung. Despite his lack of personal ambition, he manages to become, in quick succession, both a Member of Parliament and a Lord. To become an MP it is first necessary for him to fill in an application form; we learn several things from this. It seems his first name is Sodoff – he recalls how, as a child, he'd introduce himself to the other guttersnipes as Baldrick and they would say, 'Yes we know – Sodoff Baldrick'. Further questioning reveals that there is no history of sanity whatsoever in the Baldrick family, and that he can be bribed with a single turnip, possibly not even a full one. He fights to become an MP on issues rather than personality, because he hasn't got a personality. For one joyous moment, Baldrick is the proud owner of the turnip of his dreams, a snip at £400,000 (although he had to haggle).

George: Somehow he's managed to spend £59,000 on socks, yet is still unable to find a pair. Socks, he reckons, are like sex: 'Tons of it about, but I never seem to get any.' He can't say the word antidisestablishmentarianism. He becomes the leader of the Adder Party. And, at one point, he seems to turn into a chicken.

Mrs Miggins: She is ignorant of the fact that a general election has just taken place, but then, like the vast majority of the population (women, peasants, lunatics, lords, etc.), she isn't eligible to vote anyway. She helps out Mr Blackadder by turning Baldrick on the spit.

Name Checks: Lord Nelson apparently has a boat. Along with George, both Napoleon Bonaparte and geography master 'Banana-breath' Scrigshanks find themselves heading Pitt's list of enemies of the state. Chancellor Metternich was on the receiving end of the PM's cutting wit at the Congress of Strasburg when Pitt declared, 'Poo to you with knobs on!' Colin the dachshund is an inhabitant of Dunny-on-the-Wold but is ineligible to vote. Emma Hamilton's pet cat Mr Friskie dies for Blackadder's gown.

The World According to Mr Blackadder: His political opinions are a little ambivalent: while he is grateful the likes of Baldrick don't get a vote, thus preventing a resurgence of death by stoning and eating dung, he is no lover of those actually elected to power. On the one side are the fat Tory landowners, made MPs when they get to a certain weight; and on the other, raving revolutionaries. He is prepared to accept the status quo of toffs at the top and plebs at the bottom so long as he is able to make lots of cash out of both.

Essential Knowledge: Just so you know: a rotten borough is a constituency where the landowner controls the voters and MP. A robber button is something entirely different.

2: INK AND INCAPABILITY

First Broadcast: 24 September 1987.

> Dr Samuel Johnson, noted for his fat dictionary
> (Mr Robbie Coltrane)
> Byron, a Romantic junkie poet (Mr Steve Steen)
> Shelley, a Romantic junkie poet (Mr Lee Cornes)
> Coleridge, a Romantic junkie poet (Mr Jim Sweeney)

Keen to improve his reputation, George agrees to become patron of Doctor Johnson's new book, a dictionary. Blackadder is no fan of Johnson's, believing him to have disregarded his own pseudonymous novel *Edmund: A Butler's Tale*, so he is happy when George dismisses the dictionary for lack of a hero and any action. Happy, that is, until Johnson mentions the only book better than his: *Edmund: A Butler's Tale*, a work with the potential to earn its author millions. Blackadder quickly persuades George that he likes the dictionary really; the trouble is, Baldrick's put Johnson's papery thing tied up with string on to the hot orangey thing under the mantlepiecey thing – and there's no copy. Furthermore, Johnson and his entourage of Romantic poets are prepared to do bloody murder to anyone who dares lose the original. The only solution is to rewrite in one night the book that took ten years to complete, but, five hours later, Blackadder is still on 'aardvark'. He fears the worst – until George appears with the dictionary intact, albeit with a few rude words underlined. Blackadder reveals himself as the author of *Edmund*, only to find that the big papery thing that got burnt was the manuscript of his own *magnum opus*.

Watch Out For: Robbie Coltrane makes his debut as a *Blackadder* guest star. Eighties alternative comedy scene duo Steve Steen and Jim Sweeney are joined by returning guest actor and alternative comic Lee Cornes to form the poetic trio.

Cunning Plans: Baldrick's plan to scrape the soot off the remaining bits of string and replace the incinerated pages of the manuscript with new ones may not be quite as cunning as he believes. It may even be, as Blackadder alleges, 'the worst and most contemptible plan in the history of the universe'.

Cutting Comments: Blackadder maintains that the dictionary definition of the so-called genius Doctor Johnson ought to be 'a fat dullard or wobble bottom; a pompous ass with sweaty dew-flaps.'

You Horrid Little Man: After apparently burning the dictionary, Baldrick is close to discovering that an eternity in hell in the company of Beelzebub and his instruments of death is as nothing compared to five minutes with Blackadder and a pencil.

Double Entendres: When Johnson reels off a litany of big words, George is convinced that the doctor is being damned saucy; he's quite envious that he's never penultimated anyone in the solar sojourn, or even experienced any Norman tongue.

Suspiciously Modern: When Johnson announces that one book is even better than his dictionary, Blackadder wonders if England's foremost man of letters might have produced *Dictionary 2: The Return of the Killer Dictionaries*. However, Johnson is referring to *Edmund: A Butler's Tale*, which is a 'roller-coaster' novel in an age before roller-coasters. Blackadder predicts that, though George is the first person ever to use a dictionary solely for looking up rude words, he won't be the last.

Tortuous Similes: For some reason George wants to be thought 'as clever a stick in a bucket of pig swill' although he's really 'as thick as a whale omelette'. Dr Johnson is not convinced of Blackadder's powers of persuasion, believing that 'a servant who is an influence for the good is like a dog who speaks – very rare.' What's more, 'a man who can change a prince's mind is like a dog who can talk Norwegian – even rarer.' With a roaring (manuscript-fuelled) fire, George is as 'happy as a Frenchman who's invented a pair of self-removing trousers'. There is no copy of the dictionary because, in Johnson's opinion, making one would be as time-consuming and unnecessary as 'fitting wheels to a tomato'.

Blackadder: He would quite like to be a 'millionaire aristocrat with the sexual capacity of a rutting rhino'; the fact that he isn't niggles him. He has an Auntie Margery, at least in his dreams. He has spent seven years penning four hundred sizzling chapters of his epic novel, complete with hot gypsies. He deliberately winds up Dr Johnson by dropping invented words into his speech (he offers his 'most enthusiastic contrafibularities'). Fearful of being disembowelled by irate poets and having his head fed to the cat, he considers moving to Nepal to live as a goat.

Baldrick: He doesn't approve of stealing, if only because he fears going to Hell for it. He claims with some justification to be as stupid as he looks. Even so, Blackadder isn't the only person with a novel in him – Baldrick has a 'magnificent octopus' of his own, a short, semi-autobiographical work about a lovely, happy little sausage named Baldrick.

George: Some days he gets up reasonably early, at three in the afternoon. He's a member of the Naughty Hellfire Club – though apparently not a well-respected one. After having his intelligence insulted there (although having it compared to that of a donkey is possibly a compliment) he yearns to be regarded as clever. He elects to become clever by association, which is how he becomes involved with Dr Johnson and his dictionary, a book in which he believes the heroine to be the aged Mother Tongue and hopes the hero will be called

George. Hearing that it took Johnson ten years to finish his book, he sympathises: he's a bit of a slow reader himself.

Mrs Miggins: Despite Blackadder's complaint that she only sells hot water with brown grit in it, the Coffee Shoppe run by the 'lovelorn ecstasy that is Mrs Miggins' is obviously the place to be seen in London. This week it has become a literary salon, the fashionable hangout of the literati. The big-shirted, consumptive poets Lord Byron, Shelley and Coleridge have all come in veneration of Dr Johnson, and to get stoned.

Name Checks: Queenie's old friend Sir Thomas More could have avoided being burnt alive for refusing to recant his Catholicism had he only thought to say, 'I recant my Catholicism.' It is a common practice of the day for writers to assume an opposite-sex pseudonym, so in fact Mrs Radcliffe and Jane Austen are men, the latter having a beard like a rhododendron bush – though Dorothy Wordsworth has a bigger one. The only real female author is James Boswell, and she's just interested in the contents of Dr Johnson's breeches. Gerald, Lord Sandwich has devised a new snack consisting of two pieces of bread with something in between. This has been named in honour of its originator: it's called a Gerald. Lord Nelson and Lady Hamilton both get mentioned again: apparently, at the Battle of the Nile, the Admiral was heard to say, 'England knows Lady Hamilton's a virgin; poke my eye out and cut my arm off if I'm wrong.'

The World According to Mr Blackadder: He considers the dictionary to be the most pointless book since the French translation of *How to Learn French*.

Essential Knowledge: When compiling a definitive listing of English words, it is advisable not to forget 'sausage'. Not to mention 'aardvark'.

3: NOB AND NOBILITY

First Broadcast: 1 October 1987.

Lord Topper, a fop (Mr Tim McInnerny)
Lord Smedley, a fop (Mr Nigel Planer)
Ambassador, a fearsome revolutionary (Mr Chris Barrie)

Blackadder is unable to get a shepherd's pie at Mrs Miggins's Coffee Shoppe because, thanks to the daring exploits of the Scarlet Pimpernel, all things French are in vogue. Pimpernel-mania extends to the royal household, where the unimpressed Blackadder accepts a thousand-guinea wager from George's foppish friend Lord Topper to smuggle an aristo out of France and present him at the French Embassy Ball. 'Le Adder Noir' decides against a trip to France, what with it being dangerous, and instead takes it easy in the kitchen for a week before finding a pre-rescued but hard-up Frenchie at Mrs Miggins's. However, when he takes the Comte de Frou Frou to the Embassy, he finds it under the control of evil revolutionaries. When Mme Guillotine herself arrives to administer some pre-execution torture, Blackadder slips her one of Frou Frou's suicide pills, only to learn that she is George's other foppish friend, Lord Smedley, in disguise. And later, as Blackadder dazzles George with tales of his heroics in France, Frou Frou reveals himself to be Lord Topper, aka the Scarlet Pimpernel. Another suicide pill is called for, before Blackadder's deceit can be exposed. With the real Pimpernel dead, he convinces the gullible George that he was the channel-hopping hero all along, and pockets an enormous reward.

Watch Out For: A post-*Young Ones* Nigel Planer and a pre-*Red Dwarf* Chris Barrie; the latter's character apparently hung like a baby carrot and two petits pois.

Cunning Plans: Faced with death on the guillotine, Baldrick's cunning escape plan is inspired by the common farmyard chicken, which upon having its head lopped off continues to run around the yard. He suggests doing nothing until after decapitation, whereupon he and Blackadder can run around the farmyard and out of the gate to freedom.

Cutting Comments: Blackadder is scornful of the Pimpernel's achievements, finding nothing admirable in filling the city with garlic-chewing French toffs. In return, the Pimpernel – while in the guise of Lord Topper – thinks him 'the worst kind of swine' and calls him a 'lily-livered, caramel-kidneyed, custard-coloured cad'.

You Horrid Little Man: Rather than risk being exposed as a liar. Blackadder kills the Scarlet Pimpernel with one of his own suicide pills – no doubt indirectly condemning an unknown number of French aristocrats to death, too (so, not all bad then).

Double Entendres: Taken out of context, the line 'grab a few French nobs' could provoke a snigger. And, more a single entendre really, the huge suspicious sausages that have replaced 'uncouth' pies on the menu at Mrs Miggins's Coffee Shoppe are almost certainly horses' willies.

Suspiciously Modern: Lying profusely about his non-existent escapades in Revolutionary France, Blackadder claims to have climbed into Robespierre's bedroom where, along with an insulting note, he left a small tray of milk chocolates (in emulation of a certain well-known television advert). The real hero of Revolutionary France, the usually cool-headed Scarlet Pimpernel, borrows James Bond's catch-phrase when he admits to being 'shaken but not stirred.'

Tortuous Similes: Blackadder thinks the Scarlet Pimpernel is 'the most overrated human being since Judas Iscariot won the AD 31 Best Disciple Competition'. The Prince thinks his butler is 'brighter than a brain pie'.

Blackadder: His mother is still around somewhere; Blackadder has been content to let her think him dead rather than have to keep in touch with the old bat. When he learns that he's not going to be 'smacked and told not to be naughty, but basically let off' by the evil revolutionary, he plays the working-class card in an attempt to get in the good books of his 'old mucker'. He smokes a pipe.

Baldrick: He admires the Scarlet Pimpernel to the extent of sporting a repulsive-looking, false scarlet pimple on his nose by way of a tribute. He discovers that he is last in God's great

chain when an angry Blackadder kicks Mildred the cat, who
in turn pounces on a mouse, which goes for Baldrick. When
he was a youngster, the Baldrick family lived in a haunted
hovel; every night, a noxious, hairy, repulsive creature would
appear in his parents' bed. Mysteriously, the foul thing van-
ished the very day Baldrick moved away. According to
Blackadder, Pandora's Box was a misnomer: the ancient
Greeks should have labelled the container, in which all the
evils of the world were trapped, 'Baldrick's Trousers'.
Baldrick has never changed his trousers.

George: Determined not to be caught wearing boring
trousers in the presence of the Scarlet Pimpernel, he purchases what he imagines are the most magnificent pair of
trousers ever made by Messrs Snibcock and Turkey,
Courtiers to the Very Wealthy and Extremely Fat. Only, with
Blackadder away in France (i.e., hiding in the kitchen), he is
unable to put them on. George is put off going to France himself, not by the inherent danger but by the prospect of having
to wear trousers like Baldrick's. Dressed like that he feels
he'd never pull one of those 'Fabulous French birds', or even
one of the currently fashionable toothless crones who cackle
insanely and are basically playing hard to get.

Mrs Miggins: Her onion-and-garlic-bedecked Coffee
Shoppe is packed with rescued Frenchies, and the menu has
been given a Gallic flavour. Alongside snails, frogs, etc., the
French cuisine includes Chicken Pimpernel in a Scarlet
Sauce, Scarlet Chicken in a Pimpernel Sauce and, of course,
those huge suspicious sausages with Scarlet Pimpernel sauce,
which is prepared in typical French manner by squeezing a
large ripe frog . . .

Name Checks: Robespierre, the First Citizen of Revolutionary France, is included in Blackadder's completely false
account of his trip, in which case he probably doesn't count.
Meg of Bedlam Hair is allegedly Baldrick's stylist, but we
suspect that Blackadder made that up, too.

The World According to Mr Blackadder: He is unimpressed by the Pimpernel, reckoning that rescuing French

aristocrats is as easy as putting on a hat. Naturally, he hates the French – they urinate in the street and would go to bed with the kitchen sink if it was wearing a tutu. Consequently, he has no sympathy with their aristocrats going 'ooh-la-la' all the time simply because their fathers had their heads cut off. He thinks the Scarlet Pimpernel is wasting his time saving Frenchmen since the French are only there for the English to fight wars with – it's as if all those men at Agincourt died in vain, and the bloke who lit the fire under Joan of Arc wasted good matches. It seems, however, that Blackadder hasn't got such a downer on French produce, especially their wine and open fruit flans.

Essential Knowledge: In the natural world, the scarlet pimpernel is a wild plant that has small red flowers.

4: SENSE AND SENILITY

First Broadcast: 8 October 1987.

> Keanrick, a thespian (Mr Hugh Paddick)
> Mossop, a thespian (Mr Kenneth Connor)
> Anarchist (Mr Ben Elton)

Blackadder doesn't care too much for the theatre, especially when he has to go with George, who believes every word of it. The Prince thinks that two actors he has seen will be the perfect people to show him how to perform a speech Blackadder has written for him. Blackadder duly fetches Enoch Mossop and David Keanrick, who teach the Prince to stand heroically and roar – but they pour scorn on the speech, incensing its author to the point of resignation. Left to look after the household, Baldrick overhears the actors rehearsing their latest play, *The Bloody Murder of the Foul Prince Romero and his Enormous Bosomed Wife* (a philosophical work). Fearing the worst, he reports his findings to the Prince, who is convinced that they are anarchists out to kill him, currently one of his greatest fears (what with that anarchist having recently attempted to kill him). Returning home after an absence of almost five minutes, Blackadder takes charge of the situation and confirms that the actors are indeed plotting to murder the Prince; the pleading thespians are led away to certain death. Blackadder has also written a play, and there's a big part for George in *Thick Jack Clot Sits in the Stocks and Gets Pelted with Rancid Tomatoes*.

Watch Out For: Scriptwriter Ben Elton demonstrates that acting is yet another talent to add to his list. He appears as the Luddite anarchist who, as well as being against such modern inventions as the Rolling Rosalind and the Going-up-and-down-and-then-moving-along-a-bit Gertrude, is opposed to stupid Prince George and so tries to blow him up with a comedy bomb. Also, *Carry On* veteran Kenneth Connor puts in a guest appearance.

Cutting Comments: Blackadder attempts to put a proposition to Keanrick and Mossop, who assume he's trying to pick them up and berate him for thinking that because they are actors they'll sleep with everyone. Blackadder retorts with, 'I think, being actors, you are lucky to sleep with anyone.' When Blackadder 'quits', he'd like to say that he'll miss Baldrick's 'friendly companionship', but that would be a lie so he confines himself to saying, 'Sod off, and if I ever meet you again it will be twenty billion years too soon.' Baldrick's final farewell to his beloved master is a less than tearful, 'Goodbye, you lazy, big-nosed, rubber-faced bastard.'

You Horrid Little Man: Mrs Miggins unwisely calls Blackadder 'only a little butler' and receives the promise of a toasting fork in the head. Blackadder takes delight in naming the Scottish play (*Macbeth*) at every opportunity in front of the two superstitious actors, causing them to repeatedly go through a melodramatic ritual, reciting stuff about 'hot potatoes' and tweaking each other's noses. When they insult him once too often, he sees to it that they are falsely exposed as traitors, arrested and taken away to be brutally tortured and executed.

Double Entendres: Baldrick's uncle had theatrical experience: he played Macbeth's stunt codpiece in the fight scenes. 'Did he have a large part?' asks Blackadder. 'Depends who was playing Macbeth,' says Baldrick. Sometimes sophisticated wit is just no substitute for a good knob joke – hence the fact that George is naturally worried when Baldrick informs him that anarchists intend to suck on his exquisite floppily doppilies.

Tortuous Similes: Times are hard and Blackadder observes that 'disease and deprivation stalk our land like two giant stalking things'. He's also noticed a lapse in standards at the palace; it seems it's in such a dirty state that even a dung beetle that had lost interest in its career and let itself go would find it unacceptable. Keanrick and Mossop have a singular perception of the universe: their arch-enemy Blackadder is apparently not only 'as useful as fine bone china at a tea party for drunken elephants' but also 'as irritating as a potted cactus in a monkey's pyjamas'.

Blackadder: He considers a career move and he possesses the necessary attributes required to become the new King of Sardinia: specifically, he's a 'treacherous, malicious, unprincipled cad'. He claims he's had enough of working for the Prince because he's sick of having to wear the red nose and pointy hat that denote the winner of the Who's Got The Stupidest Master competition every year at the Guild of Butlers' Christmas Party. However, a slip of the tongue confirms the true nature of the master and servant relationship in the Royal Household – Blackadder admits that he's glad to be back in the saddle, when of course he really meant harness. He doesn't much like being referred to as Bladder, and he really hates being called Mr Hopelessly-Drivello-Can't-Write-For-Toffee-Crappy-Butler-Weed. If anything, he'd quite like to be known as Mr Brilliantly-Undervalued-Butler-Who-Hasn't-Had-a-Raise-For-a-Fortnight. According to Baldrick, Mr B's motto is 'When the going gets tough, the tough hide under the table.'

Baldrick: Blackadder doubts Baldrick's ability to replace him and fulfil the role of butler without a passing surgeon cutting open his head with a spade and putting in a new brain, but the ambitious dogsbody is fine with that option. Despite having an uncle who once appeared in a play, the theatre doesn't impress him with all its sex and violence. He can get that at home. Except for the sex.

George: Unable to distinguish between real life and the events taking place in a play, he still hasn't got over the shock of witnessing the fatal stabbing of Julius Caesar. He is ignorant of the hardships faced by the oppressed masses; Blackadder has to remind him that some people are so poor they are 'forced to have children simply to provide a cheap alternative to turkey at Christmas'. Worried about being overthrown, he takes Baldrick for an oppressed mass. Believe it or not, George once had a brilliant idea. It involved wearing underwear outside his trousers to save on laundry bills.

Mrs Miggins: The Coffee Shoppe gets all theatrical, and there's more Shakespearean dialogue than buns when London's luvvies call in on their way to rehearsals.

Name Checks: Once reassured that Caesar hasn't really been murdered, George becomes convinced he's seen three blokes bump off an actor called Kemp. As well as Napoleon Bonaparte's plea for a King of Sardinia, the Situations Vacant column reveals that Mr and Mrs Pitt require a babyminder for Pitt the Younger and Stephenson wants marketing assistance with the moving kettle he's invented.

The World According to Mr Blackadder: Blackadder is mindful of the current changeable state of world politics and the precarious situation facing the remaining monarchies. Already America has won her independence, France has disposed of her King, and now there are rumblings in Prussia, though that's most likely due to the sausages. He warns George that across the world the cry is 'Peace, freedom and a few less fat bastards eating all the pie' – no doubt completely spoiling the Prince's enjoyment of the pie he's eating at the time. He didn't realise that actors rehearsed; he thought 'they just got drunk, stuck on silly hats and trusted to luck'.

Essential Knowledge: When first seen, the actors Keanrick and Mossop are performing in a play at Drury Lane. Both are dressed in Egyptian garb when Keanrick's character unconvincingly kills Mossop's with a short sword. Taking all this into account, the production seems strangely reminiscent of *The Death of the Pharaoh!* in 'Born to be King'.

5: AMY AND AMIABILITY

First Broadcast: 15 October 1987.

Amy Hardwood, the elusive Shadow
(Miss Miranda Richardson)
Mr Hardwood, her father
(Mr Warren Clarke)
Sally Cheapside, a young lady of doubtful virtue
(Miss Barbara Horne)
The Duke of Cheapside (Mr Roger Avon)

The bills have arrived and Blackadder is skint. Baldrick suggests he becomes a dashing highwayman like the Shadow, but he doesn't fancy getting hanged and has a better idea anyway. Unfortunately, his usual source of funding, George, is broke too, having blown all his cash playing cards. Blackadder persuades him to get money by marrying into it; trouble is, he can't find a suitable girl. Then, the ideal matrimonial candidate arrives in town: Amy Hardwood, daughter of a noted industrialist. With Blackadder's much-needed assistance, the coarse, unrefined Prince goes a-wooing the delicate and fluffy Amy. Mr Hardwood agrees to the marriage, so that he and his daughter will no longer be poor and hungry. And, with this revelation, the wedding is cancelled. Turning to highway robbery after all, Blackadder encounters the elusive, squirrel-hating Shadow who, to his surprise, insists on a kiss. The Shadow turns out to be Amy, not so fluffy after all. She persuades Blackadder to return to the palace and rob it, so they can go off together, but it's a double-cross. Thanks to Baldrick's desire for the Shadow's autograph, though, Blackadder turns the tables and claims the reward for turning in his erstwhile partner.

Watch Out For: Warren Clarke, who plays plain-speaking Lancashire industrialist Mr Hardwood, is one of television's busiest actors, although he's probably now best known as the plain-speaking half of the Yorkshire-based detective duo *Dalziel and Pascoe*.

Cunning Plans: Although he has no desire to be hanged for wearing a silly hat, desperation and a lack of cash ensure that, for once, Blackadder follows Baldrick's guidance and becomes a daring highwayman.

Cutting Comments: Blackadder refers to George as 'an arrogant, half-German yob with a mad dad'. An encounter with Blackadder the highwayman transforms the Duke of Cheapside from the doting father of a spoilt daughter who could do no wrong to a man who denounces his girl as a 'pregnant junkie fag hag'. Blackadder informs Mrs Miggins that 'if we were the last three people on Earth, I would be trying to start a family with Baldrick.'

You Horrid Little Man: Surprisingly, after committing a robbery with Baldrick, Blackadder divides the loot down the middle. Then he proceeds to rob Baldrick at gunpoint, which is more like it.

Double Entendres: As soon as capital punishment is mentioned, it becomes inevitable that someone will make a comment about being well hung.

Suspiciously Modern: Before he can shout 'Hi-yo, Quicksilver!' again, Blackadder finds himself on 'an unrealistic grassy knoll' facing certain death at the hands of a woman who apparently has access to some kind of voice-altering device. Oh yes, there's also that bit where Blackadder drops a tray when he thinks he's been found out, but it jumps back into his hands when it turns out he isn't suspected of being Amy's accomplice after all. This was achieved by reversing the video and, of course, even simple video effects weren't available in the eighteenth century.

Tortuous Similes: Blackadder is unable to lend George any money as he's 'as poor as a church mouse that's just had an enormous tax bill on the very day his wife ran off with another mouse, taking all the cheese.'

Blackadder: He suspects his hairdo to be slightly effeminate. Intending to start a new life in the West Indies, he purchases a bathing costume and forty gallons of coconut oil. He has a degree of fighting ability and is easily able to floor George. He may well be an expert horseman, too, but thanks to, among other things, the dreaded Horse Plague of Old London Town, we only see him ride Baldrick.

Baldrick: He once attempted to solve the problem of his mother's low ceiling by cutting her head off. Though he doesn't know the difference between concubines and porcupines, he's not entirely stupid. For one thing, he knows what irony is: it's like goldy and bronzey only it's made out of iron. Highwaymen, and the Shadow in particular, have replaced the Scarlet Pimpernel as the objects of his fan worship. He collects the memorabilia, keeps a scrapbook and would love to obtain the Shadow's autograph. Baldrick gets a lot closer to a highwayman than even he could imagine when he becomes Blackadder's faithful steed, Quicksilver. If Blackadder ever establishes his plantation in Barbados, he will send for Baldrick who, for once, will stand out as an individual – being the only white slave amidst all the black ones.

George: He was given five grand by Parliament to drink himself to death with, but he gambled it away, believing that the object of playing cards is to lose money. He is initially reluctant to get hitched, as he believes it will restrict his roaring, rogering, gorging and puking. Blackadder assures him that all are considered perfectly acceptable within wedlock in the eyes of the modern church. George likes girls who are lovers, laughers, dancers and, adds Blackadder, 'bonkers'. There is no argument from the Prince, who by repute has the manners of a boy cow's dingle-dangle. Blackadder has to write his love poems for him, as George's are a little uncouth.

Mrs Miggins: She confesses to Blackadder that she's always hoped they'd get married and wait for the slither of little Adders. It breaks her heart when Blackadder fails to reciprocate the feelings.

Name Checks: Mr Harwood patented a machine called the Ravelling Nancy. Donning a black highwayman's outfit, Blackadder tells Baldrick that he's auditioning for Arnold the Bat in Sheridan's new play; Baldrick believes him, so he doesn't know what irony is after all. Due to his involvement in a purple pants probe, the Regency dandy Beau Brummel makes the pages of *The Times*. Lady Hamilton apparently disproves the theory that it isn't possible to make money out of looks and charm alone. Of the women available to marry George, Sophia of Turin isn't likely to want to as she's met him – and Princess Caroline of Brunswick is reputed to have the worst personality in Germany, which, if true, is quite some achievement. Had Amy married the Prince, it wouldn't have been the first time that class boundaries were crossed in her family. There was her Uncle Ted and Aunty Dot – he was a pig poker and she was the Duchess of Argyll. And Aunty Ruth, the milkmaid, married Uncle Isaiah, who was the Pope.

The World According to Mr Blackadder: He fails to see why common thieves should be idolised just because they ride horses. Giving out sound advice, he warns Baldrick against going to Wales: 'a ghastly place. Huge sinewy men roam the valleys terrifying people with their close harmony singing.' Baldrick is further advised never to ask for directions there. 'You need half a pint of phlegm in your throat just to pronounce the place names . . . you'll be washing spit out of your hair for a fortnight.'

Essential Knowledge: This episode was originally entitled 'Cape and Capability', and was even listed as such in *Radio Times*.

6: DUEL AND DUALITY

First Broadcast: 22 October 1987.

The Duke of Wellington, a famous soldier (Mr Stephen Fry)
King George III, a mad monarch (Mr Gertan Klauber)

Blackadder's violent, Scottish, look-a-like cousin MacAdder
is down for a visit and a spot of insurrection. Meanwhile,
after a night of passion with a pair of Wellingtons, George
finds he's put his foot in it when the Duke of Wellington
decides to kill him for taking advantage of his nieces. Blackadder offers to fight a duel in the Prince's place, but intends
to have MacAdder stand in for him. So, when Wellington
visits, George and Blackadder have to switch identities.
Unfortunately, MacAdder doesn't fancy the duel, even for
enough money to buy the Outer Hebrides (fourteen shillings
and sixpence), so Blackadder decides to let George fight his
own battles after all – until he is bribed into reconsidering.
The duel is fought with cannon, and, as Blackadder reads the
instructions, Wellington fires. Blackadder seems mortally
wounded, but his life is saved by a cigarillo case that
Wellington gave to him. The Duke decides that justice has
been done and, when George arrives claiming to be the real
Prince, he shoots him dead for his impertinence. Even mad
King George III can't tell Blackadder apart from his son,
which enables him to step into the Prince's shoes
permanently.

Watch Out For: Sometime *Carry On* actor Gertan Klauber
becomes the latest *Blackadder* actor to play a reigning
monarch when King George III finally puts in an appearance
– and what a nutcase he is (the King, that is, not Gertan
Klauber). He wants his son to marry a rosebush, and he fin-
ishes every sentence with the word 'penguin'. Oh, and
Rowan Atkinson turns up in a guest-starring role as red-
wigged lunatic MacAdder. Hmm, perhaps there's something
in that idea about Donald, Duke of Argyll being a Blackadder
after all; if the family tree still has a Scottish branch . . .

Cunning Plans: It is Baldrick who comes up with the idea for someone to stand in for the Prince and fight the duel – quite a good idea, in fact. But it's also Baldrick who puts Blackadder's name forward – and that's not such a good idea at all. Blackadder's own adjunct to the cunning plan has MacAdder fighting the duel for him: a fine plan, but one that turns out to have one tiny drawback.

Cutting Comments: Blackadder hates it when MacAdder turns up: 'he's such a frog-eyed, beetle-browed basket case.' His exclamation to the Prince, 'You're going to die, fat pig!' is, under the circumstances, perhaps just a little too mean. At least Mrs Miggins only talks about George's smelly feet and calls him a 'fat Prussian truffle pig' behind his back – or so she thinks.

You Horrid Little Man: A disguised Blackadder seizes the opportunity to join Wellington in the jolly sport of repeatedly beating up Prince George.

Suspiciously Modern: Blackadder, who wants to be remembered, hopes that, hundreds of years hence, episodes from his life will be played out weekly at 9.30 by a great heroic actor of the age. Baldrick shares his passion, and imagines that he might be played by 'some tiny tit in a beard'. Mrs Miggins makes an allusion to the difficulties of modern-day split-screen techniques when she points out that Blackadder and MacAdder keep missing each other – 'I can't imagine why.'

Tortuous Similes: Blackadder hates being likened to his Scottish cousin, believing them to be 'as similar as two completely dissimilar things in a pod'. He accuses MacAdder of being 'madder than Mad Jack McMad, the winner of this year's Mr Madman competition.'

Blackadder: He has been looking after the Prince since they were babies and he had to show George which part of his mother was serving the drinks. He'd mud-wrestle his own mother for 'a ton of cash, an amusing clock and a sack of French porn'. Looking suspiciously like Blackadder in a wig is MacAdder, a cousin from north of the border, 'the most dangerous man to wear a skirt in Europe' and an obvious graduate of the Russ Abbott academy of mad, ginger-haired Scotsmen. Fortune vomits on Blackadder's eiderdown once more, when MacAdder refuses to fight in his stead. Ultimately, though, after centuries in the wilderness, it seems that a Blackadder might once more become King of England. This time, he might even hold on to the throne for more than a few seconds.

Baldrick: Calling MacAdder a knock-kneed Scottish pillock earns him a punch in the mouth. His mother is indirectly responsible, having once told him to stand up to homicidal maniacs; since this is the same mother who believes him to be a tall, handsome stallion of a man, he ought to have known better. Baldrick loves his mum. Another of his kinfolk is Bert Baldrick, the dogsbody to Mr Gainsborough's butler. Bert says that Gainsborough's portraits are similar 'since they are painted to a romantic ideal, rather than as a true depiction of the idiosyncratic facial qualities of the person in question'. Baldrick has been known to write the odd poem about the Prince, and – insult of insults! – thinks of him as a clot.

George: He dies.

Mrs Miggins: Dazzled by MacAdder's prowess with his weapon, she elects to leave her Coffee Shoppe behind and go with him to Scotland, where the kippers roam free. Once there, she intends to fight MacAdder's woman Morag in the traditional Highland manner: bare-breasted and each carrying an eight-pound baby. It is a fight in which she will undoubtedly be killed.

Name Checks: George's father, the King, is suffering from the delusion that he's a small village in Lincolnshire, so Wellington passes on news of his campaign to the Prince instead. Napoleon is in North Africa, while Nelson waits in Alaska in case Bonaparte should attempt an attack via the North Pole. Blackadder suggests that Trafalgar might be a better venue for Nelson's fleet. Along with Morag, the mighty Clan MacAdder consists of Jamie and Angus, who are both fine boys – apart from Angus, who's a girl. Mr

McNulty has a particularly difficult bloater, which he needs shifting by MacAdder the fishmonger.

The World According to MacAdder: MacAdder would gladly pretend to be the Duke of Wellington and kill the Prince of Wales, as then he'd be king and crowned with the ancient stone bonnet of MacAdder. But as for duelling with the Iron Duke, well, he'd rather sleep with the Loch Lomond Monster.

Essential Knowledge: Not surprisingly in the least, the *Blackadder* interpretation of Wellington is at odds with our own historical research (we watched some episodes of *Sharpe*), which revealed that the Duke was opposed to duelling – with cannons in particular, we shouldn't wonder. The makers of the film *Sabotage*, however, must have considered Fry's portrayal totally authentic as they asked him to recreate the role in their movie. There's probably a pun to be found there about giving it more Welly, but we can't think of one.

Special Editions

During the gap between *Blackadder the Third* and *Blackadder Goes Forth*, two special episodes were broadcast on the BBC. Between them they introduced three more members of the Blackadder dynasty (some may argue that it was four, but two of them were the same only under different circumstances, so there).

The Cavalier Years

For the benefit of anyone who's been off the planet for the last fifteen years, the fund-raising Comic Relief was created in 1985 as the comedians' response to the Ethiopian famine that had already inspired musicians to form Band Aid. Celebrity-packed live shows, a number one record by Cliff Richard and the Young Ones and a tie-in book all helped to make it a big success. Comic Relief continues to raise money for worthy causes to this day, with Richard Curtis as one of its prime movers.

In 1988, Comic Relief launched the first of what would become its biannual Red Nose Days. Throughout the day, people were encouraged to take part in all kinds of mad events in order to raise money, most involving baked beans. The more reserved members of society were able to put money into the coffers by purchasing official merchandise in the form of red noses (each subsequent Red Nose Day would have its own unique red nose – there have been waving noses, tomato noses, furry noses and squeaky noses – and a full set is as desirable as a *Blue Peter* badge). The day culminated in an evening-long telethon broadcast live on BBC 1.

Amidst the silliness, a number of pre-recorded segments were featured, one of which was a new mini-episode of *Blackadder*.

Over the years, such specially made – and often star-studded – Comic Relief editions of popular TV comedies have proven to be audience favourites on the night. Shows such as *The Vicar of Dibley*, *Men Behaving Badly* and *The Brittas Empire* have all had the treatment. Usually, though, these specials – which are essentially extended sketches – are separate entities that don't necessarily fit into the continuity of the programmes they are derived from. Uniquely, *Blackadder – The Cavalier Years* served to expand the mythology of the source material. Which was nice.

The Cavalier Years is a bit of a misnomer. *Blackadder – The Cavalier Fifteen Minutes* would have been nearer the mark. But the title does provide a clue to the historical setting of this glimpse into the life of yet another of the infamous line. For the first time, a Blackadder is introduced out of chronological sequence, as the family history is backdated from the Georgian era to the English Civil War where, as per usual, the Edmund Blackadder of the age (Rowan Atkinson, if it needed saying) can be found hobnobbing with royalty.

If King Charles I is an oddly familiar character, it's because Stephen Fry portrays him as a playful parody of the latter-day Charles, Prince of Wales. Warren Clarke appears as the period's other major player, Oliver Cromwell. Both are perfectly suited to their roles, so it was convenient that both had recently guest-starred in *Blackadder the Third* and were available to continue their association for this one-off short. Tony Robinson's portrayal of Baldrick isn't significantly different from his previous one – though, strictly speaking, the 'previous one' could be the one from *Blackadder II* or the one from *Blackadder the Third*, depending on whether your opinion is based on historical or broadcast chronology. Either way, he's pretty much the same.

Comedian Harry Enfield also lends his support by stepping into Patrick Allen's long-deserted shoes as the *Blackadder* narrator. He sets the scene for this episode, which opens in

Blackadder Hall, the home of Sir Edmund. Much of the story takes place in the Hall's kitchen, which looks rather a lot like a redressed version of Prince George's kitchen, in fact. The rest occurs in the King's bed chamber in the Tower of London (thankfully, the execution scene takes place off camera and is only heard).

It is probably not worth venturing an opinion as to whether the English Civil War, Oliver Cromwell, etc. could have provided enough comedy material to fill an entire six-part series of *Blackadder*. From the outset, the possibility of follow-up episodes could be ruled out due to the fact that *The Cavalier Years* was constructed as the concluding chapter to that particular period in history (although both Atkinson and Fry would briefly revisit the period a decade later, as we'll see in Chapter 7).

Exclusive Relief

Nowadays, it has to be said, there are certain uncharitable people who set the video while Comic Relief is on, thoughtlessly go down the pub and then watch the funny bits later on. Let us be charitable and hope that they didn't inadvertently fast forward past *The Cavalier Years* on the first Red Nose night, otherwise they'd have missed a gem. For anyone whose drinking habits did preclude a viewing first time around, the episode made its way onto the Comic Relief video *Exclusive Relief* in 1991. The tape also includes 'Goodbyeee', billed as the final episode of the Blackadder Chronicles; a red-nosed Captain Blackadder and Baldrick from *Blackadder Goes Forth* are depicted on the sleeve. Incidentally, in *Night of the Comic Dead*, another sketch on the video, Phil Cool impersonates the ghost of Charles I.

In the USA, *The Cavalier Years* was thoughtfully included at the end of a *Blackadder II* video, putting it in its rightful sequential place. Over here, a rumoured appearance on a tape with *Blackadder's Christmas Carol* never materialised. Which leads us nicely into . . .

A Christmas Carol

Christmas is a time for traditional things: snogging under the
mistletoe at the office party (with someone you don't really
fancy, so you'll be deeply embarrassed about it come New
Year), drinking until you puke, family bickering, sprouts and
sticking fifteen minutes on to sit coms and calling them Festive Specials. This is really all that needs to be said about the
origins of *Blackadder's Christmas Carol*.

If one or two episodes of *Blackadder the Third* had their
roots in English literature, then this Christmas special has the
whole bloody tree. Like the Bill Murray movie *Scrooged*
(though, come to think of it, not actually like it at all) the
episode is a disparate take on Charles Dickens' famous tale *A
Christmas Carol*, with one Ebenezer Blackadder filling in for
the infamous miser Ebenezer Scrooge. Of course, simply
substituting a typical Blackadder for Scrooge – who, like the
skinflint mentioned in the episode, wouldn't think twice
about using his John Thomas as a draught excluder – would
have been all too easy. So unlike his ancestors, the Victorian-
age Blackadder was altruistic, philanthropic and quite the
nicest man in all England. Well, at least that's how he started
out.

In this version of the story, the Spirit of Christmas, in the
form of Robbie Coltrane, turns up and uses visions to show
Ebenezer how, throughout history, other members of the family turned being selfish and cunning to their advantage. While
Robbie Coltrane is great in the role, there is no actual reason
for the Spirit of Christmas's interest in Blackadder. It might
have been more logical to have Rowan Atkinson play the
ghost of one of the earlier Blackadders who materialises in
order to persuade Ebenezer to mend his benevolent ways.
However, if there's one thing this special isn't short of, it's
Blackadders. The vision plot device allows the inclusion of
self-contained vignettes revisiting characters from the second
and third series. Conspicuous by its absence, however, is any
mention of the original; if Ebenezer was the white sheep of
the dynasty then, in some quarters, the first was obviously

still regarded as the black sheep (also noticeably absent in the Elizabethan segment is Tim McInnerny's Percy, as it were).

In exchange, however, the episode gives us a glimpse of a distant future – well, in fact, two distant futures – and two possible destinies for Ebenezer's family. Despite its introduction of two new Blackadders to the canon, the space-age segment is the least enjoyable of the three. This is perhaps due in part to the characters being both unfamiliar and undeveloped – but, aside from the sight of Baldrick in a posing pouch, which is quite amusing, it is too reliant on the belief that pseudo-sci-fi jargon in itself is funny.

As well as recreating their familiar *Blackadder* characters for the retrospectives, Stephen Fry, Hugh Laurie, Patsy Byrne and Miranda Richardson turn up as futuristic counterparts, Richardson's Queen Asphixia looking particularly gorgeous in a long, tight-curled wig that is surpassed only by Admiral Blackadder's own.

The special's cast is also augmented by several actors who had previous *Blackadder* experience. The aforementioned Robbie Coltrane had, of course, been Dr Johnson the previous year, and his list of other credits is almost as big as Johnson's dictionary. We've already mentioned his appearances alongside Ben Elton as part of the *Alfresco* team, while devotees of uncompromising drama probably associate him more with the hard-living Fitz in Granada's *Cracker*. His international reputation also keeps on growing, thanks, among other things, to his appearances in the 007 franchise.

Representing royalty for the contemporaneous sections of the piece were Miriam Margolyes and Jim Broadbent, reunited for the first time since the original series episode 'The Queen of Spain's Beard'. Margolyes, who almost became Mrs Black Adder (Mrs Plantagenet, actually) in her debut appearance, had also portrayed the puritanical Lady Whiteadder in 'Beer'. Though no relation this time, her role here – Queen Victoria, the monarch of the age – is just as important in *Blackadder* terms.

In something of a promotion from his days as the Spanish Infanta's translator, Broadbent became Prince Albert. He's become something of a movie star since then, what with his appearances in *The Borrowers* and in *The Avengers* (as Mother) – and he picked up the Best Actor Award at the 1999 Venice Film Festival for his portrayal of the Gilbert half of Gilbert and Sullivan.

Broadbent also appeared semi-regularly in *Only Fools and Horses*, as did New Zealand-born actor Denis Lill. Lill, previously the red-faced fat git Sir Talbot Buxomly in 'Dish and Dishonesty', was now cast as the red-faced fat git Beadle. In real life, he's neither fat nor a git, and he's appeared in lots of stuff, both dramatic and funny, including *The Survivors*, *Outside Edge* and *The 10%ers*.

The special's jaunt back to the Georgian era allows the inclusion of a historical celebrity for whom there hadn't been any room in *Blackadder the Third*, although he rated several passing mentions. The Admiral Lord Nelson was played by Philip Pope, who was also Leonardo Acropolis in 'Money'. Pope, a musician as well as a comic actor, was one of the guiding lights behind the Hee Bee Gee Bees and, of course, one of Tony Robinson's *Who Dares Wins* cronies. Nelson's appearance, however, is little more than a cameo – he wakes from a doze believing he's gone blind, but in fact he has his patch over the wrong eye.

As usual, Howard Goodall was responsible for the music, this time providing a Christmassy choral arrangement. Speaking to the *Red Dwarf Smegazine* (to us, as it happens), he recalled that the episode almost had its own piece of spin-off merchandise: 'We wrote a song about Baldrick to come out over Christmas, but the lyrics were just too rude so it sort of died a death.' Quite right too: Ebenezer certainly wouldn't have approved.

Watching *The Cavalier Years* is like dipping into a larger saga, but there is a sense of completeness about *Blackadder's Christmas Carol*. Ebenezer's liberation from goodness works well as a self-contained story – although, for someone as nice as he is reputed to be, he turns bad surprisingly quickly and easily. If anything he's worse than the other Blackadders, who at least waited until poor Baldrick had done something to warrant a punch in the face before they punched him in the face. Having said that, it is satisfying to watch Ebenezer's settling of scores against those appalling people who'd taken advantage of him in the past. In Blackadder's distaff world, the resolution is satisfactory. Even if his first attempts at self-ishness don't all go to plan, he's bound to improve with practice.

The sleeve of the video release reveals some interesting facts about the episode. For example, it wasn't filmed on location in Barbados, Kenya or New Zealand; and Baldrick's Posing Pouch appears by kind permission of Orthopaedic Maggot Hammocks (Ipswich) Ltd. Nicola Bryant's character is here credited as 'Awful Screeching Woman' and is apparently based on a real person (living or dead). Though, if everyone else is 'fictional and imaginary', does that mean Queen Victoria, Prince Albert, Lord Nelson, etc. never existed?

The Blackadder Specials

Written by Richard Curtis and Ben Elton;
produced by John Lloyd.
Blackadder's Christmas Carol directed by Richard Boden.

BLACKADDER – THE CAVALIER YEARS

First Broadcast: 5 February 1988.

Sir Edmund Blackadder (Rowan Atkinson)
Baldrick (Tony Robinson)
Charles I (Stephen Fry)
Oliver Cromwell (Warren Clarke)

Blackadder Hall, November 1648. King Charles I is spending the winter in a blackcurrant bush, hiding from his pursuers, when Oliver Cromwell arrives looking for Royalist scum. Baldrick almost manages not to give the King away. In the Tower of London, Charles isn't unduly worried, since no jury will convict him. However, he is found guilty of treason and sentenced to death. His loyal chum Blackadder assures him that no man in the land will come forward to carry out the execution. Wrong again. But who would be so low and depraved as to take on the task? And what is Baldrick's new job . . .? In the event, it's Blackadder who gets to wear the executioner's hood, while Baldrick has to concoct a good excuse for his master's apparent absence. There's a bit of a hiccup, though, when Charles recognises his executioner's voice. Though the likelihood of success is zero, Blackadder attempts one of Baldrick's cunning plans. He offers an eager crowd not the King's head but rather a plausible alternative. But they see through his ruse, and he's forced to kill the King as planned, change sides and hand both Baldrick and Charles's infant son over to the Roundheads.

Watch Out For: Warren Clarke already had a *Blackadder* credit on his CV, thanks to his memorable portrayal of Mr Hardwood in 'Amy and Amiability'. A pretty obvious doll stands in for the baby prince.

Cunning Plans: As Blackadder predicted, the crowd immediately see the difference between the head of a traitor and a huge pumpkin with a pathetic moustache drawn on it.

Cutting Comments: Oliver Cromwell, in Blackadder's view, 'has so many warts on his face, it's only when he sneezes you find out which one is his nose.'

You Horrid Little Man: Sir Edmund agrees to execute his dear friend the King when he finds out how much the job pays. He's too busy to punch Baldrick, so instead he proffers his fist for his servant to run into face first. He also kills an ant to make a point.

Double Entendres: Sir Edmund is worried about the fix he's in. 'Something will pop up,' says Baldrick. 'Not under Puritanism it won't,' Blackadder replies.

Suspiciously Modern: So, that's *King* Charles then, is it? Also, Baldrick produces a pumpkin that he's prepared earlier, in imitation of *Blue Peter*.

Tortuous Similes: The King is as likely to be caught as 'a fox being chased by a pack of one-legged tortoises'. Or so Blackadder tells him, and he might be lying. Baldrick's head, he reckons, is 'as empty as a eunuch's underpants', perhaps because his brain is 'like the four-headed, man-eating haddock fish beast of Aberdeen – it doesn't exist'. As a consequence, Baldrick's family's record in the cunning plan department is 'about as impressive as Stumpy Oleg

McNoleg's personal best in the Market Harborough Marathon'.

Blackadder: The only surviving member of the Blackadder dynasty, Sir Edmund, is resident at Blackadder Hall. He is also the one man who has remained loyal to the King, although he often lies to him. He comes to realise that, in the 'one measly Civil War in the entire history of England', he's chosen 'the wrong bloody side'. While on the wrong (i.e., the Royalist) side, he is dark-haired with a beard and moustache; when he switches to the Puritan cause, he becomes blond and clean shaven.

Baldrick: He is the son of a pig farmer and a bearded lady. His singing has the entertainment value of a tap-dancing oyster, and he loves chops. He's not quite the evil bastard that he seems: though he takes on the job of executioner, he intends to use his fee to buy a new king. He ate his family inheritance ages ago: it was £50.

Charles I: Not that he wants to be executed, but he finds it disheartening that no young people can be found to do the deed. All they need, he believes, is initiative, which is what his award scheme is all about. When Oliver Cromwell informs him that he spells his doom, the King is encouraged that someone can actually spell. It saddens him that many people can't spell nowadays, particularly in the inner cities, which are of special interest. When Blackadder gets in to visit him by dressing as a priest, the King finds that the 'perverted' disguise reminds him of school. With the end in sight, he looks forward to meeting his maker. He enjoys meeting people from all walks of life, particularly manufacturing.

Oliver Cromwell: He strokes Baldrick's hair and calls him 'my proud beauty'. The man is obviously insane.

Name Checks: Thomas More gets yet another name check when, his identity 'hidden' by his hood, Blackadder can't resist telling the doomed King how generously More tipped his executioner. Charles, who thought service was included, isn't so generous – so Blackadder reminds him of the Earl of

Essex and the ballad they still sing about him down the Chepstow Arms: 'The Earl he had a thousand sovereigns, hey nonny no. He gave them all away to the man with the axe-o.'

The World According to Sir Edmund Blackadder: He doesn't relish the prospect of the end of the monarchy. He fears that England will enter a hideous age of Puritanism, which will see the closure of theatres and lace hankies for men made illegal.

Essential Information: Blackadder can't be with the King on the day of his execution because 'his wife's sister's puppy fell into the strawberry patch'.

BLACKADDER'S CHRISTMAS CAROL

First Broadcast: 23 December 1988.

Blackadders (Rowan Atkinson)
Baldricks (Tony Robinson)
The Spirit of Christmas (Robbie Coltrane)
Queens Elizabeth I/Asphixia IX (Miranda Richardson)
Princes Regent/Pigmot (Hugh Laurie)
Lords Melchett/Frondo (Stephen Fry)
Nursie/Bernard (Patsy Byrne)
Queen Victoria (Miriam Margolyes)
Prince Albert (Jim Broadbent)
Mrs Scratchit (Pauline Melville)
Beadle (Denis Lill)
Millicent (Nicola Bryant)
Ralph (Ramsay Gilderdale)
Enormous Orphans
(David Nunn, David Barber, Erkan Mustapha)
Lord Nelson (Philip Pope)

Christmas Eve: the moustache shop of Ebenezer Blackadder, a generous and compassionate man whose soft heart makes him a soft touch for the locals – from a collection of enormous orphans to criminal genius Mrs Scratchit and his

own goddaughter Millicent. Retiring to bed, Ebenezer
receives a visitation from the Spirit of Christmas, who's just
passing through on his rounds. Surprised to learn that his
ancestors were stinkers, he requests a vision and sees his
Elizabethan ancestor outwit Lord Melchett with a novelty
death warrant from a Christmas cracker. Intrigued, he then
witnesses his Regency ancestor take advantage of Prince
George's fondness for sad, lonely old grannies in order to
acquire his mammoth collection of presents. Ebenezer
wonders what would happen if he himself was bad. A
glimpse at Christmas Future reveals that his descendant will
rule the universe – whereas, if he stays good, then the space-
age Blackadder's fate will be to wear Baldrick's posing
pouch. A blacker Blackadder rises on Christmas Day, and
proceeds to vent his wrath upon those who've taken advantage of his previous good nature – including the dumpy
woman and the Glaswegian with the German accent who
come visiting. Alas, he fails to recognise Queen Victoria and
Prince Albert, come to reward him for his virtuousness with
£50,000 and the title Baron Blackadder.

Watch Out For: Nicola Bryant first came to the attention of
viewers as *Doctor Who* girl Peri. Sadly, the Victorian apparel
she wears keeps her impressive figure well under wraps.
Playing her beau, Ralph, is Ramsey Gilderdale, who would
later join Tony Robinson on the baddies' side in *Maid Marian
and her Merry Men*. One of the orphans in danger of
exploding and showering Blackadder with two dozen semi-
digested pies is Erkan Mustapha, who'd been the much-
bullied Roland Browning in *Grange Hill*. Another is David
Nunn, the rotund semi-regular messenger from the first
series.

Cunning Plans: The Elizabethan Blackadder devises a
subtle plan instead of the usual cunning one. It involves using
a bit of reverse psychology on Melchett to get him to give the
Queen, currently in an anti-Christmas frame of mind, a big
pressie. Unfortunately, the plan backfires when the Queen
has a sudden change of heart; he really should have opted for
a cunning plan.

Cutting Comments: Baldrick is looking forward to a wet kiss for Christmas, but Blackadder thinks the only way he is likely to get a wet kiss is to make a pass at a water closet – and that's when he's still nice Ebenezer. After his conversion, he refers to Victoria as Queen Piglet Features and declares her the winner of the Round Britain Shortest, Fattest, Dumpiest Woman Competition – and Albert the winner of the Stupidest Accent Award. Although, in Blackadder's opinion, Millicent's head is emptier than a hermit's address book, at least she thought to bring the fish course with her, in the form of her boyfriend Ralph.

You Horrid Little Man: Baldrick believes that the most loving Christmas presents are those that are handmade by the giver; which is just as well because Ebenezer makes him a fist. What is so thoughtful about the gift is that it is one that can be used over and over again, as Blackadder demonstrates. For sheer horridness, the Regency Blackadder resorting to mugging an old lady will take some beating.

Double Entendres: When nice Mr Blackadder talks about size not being important and adds, 'It's not what you've got, it's where you stick it,' he is, of course, talking about his rather diminutive Christmas twig. His exclamation 'Baste my steaming puddings!' sounds a bit rude, too, as does 'Peel my tangerines!'

Suspiciously Modern: In order to show Ebenezer the sheer awfulness of his ancestors, the Spirit of Christmas is certain he'll have to show him the full one-hour-ten vision with a break and ice cream. Conversely, Pigmot's looking forward to watching *20,000 Years of the Two Ronnoids* now seems suspiciously dated.

Blackadder: Christened Ebenezer instead of the more commonly used Edmund, the Victorian Blackadder owns a moustache shop on Pudding Lane. He doesn't laugh at toilet humour and, by repute, he is the nicest man in the land. The Elizabethan and Regency Blackadders with whom we are already familiar (and therefore, by implication, the Black Adder) are his direct ancestors – and, as he's the only surviving member of the Blackadder dynasty, he must in turn be a direct ancestor (grandfather?) of Captain Edmund Blackadder. Upon learning that, if he becomes bad, his descendant – Grand Admiral of the Dark Segment and Lord of the High Slung Bottoms of Zob, aka Blackadder, thrice-endowed donkey of the trouser pod – will rule the universe, he mends his good ways and lets the dark side of his personality come to the fore.

Baldrick: The Victorian Baldrick is a man of faith and, like his Regency ancestor, believes in the Big Pink Pixie in the Sky. He can't spell too well and, perhaps uniquely, manages to get every single letter wrong in Christmas. If anything, though, his mathematical ability is even worse: according to his calculation, seventeen pounds and a penny minus seventeen pounds equals thirty-eight pounds, eight shillings and four pence. If Ebenezer were to embrace goodness again then one of Baldrick's descendants could become Grand Marshall of the Smells, leader of Earth's Imperial Navy, ultimately responsible for the security of our planet. So, everyone would be fucked, basically. As for his ancestors, well, the Regency Baldrick gets dragged up again – this time as a sweet old (bearded) lady.

Queen Victoria: She likes to go out amongst her subjects at Christmas and reward the virtuous. Another thing she likes at Christmas is a goose. That's another double entendre, isn't it?

Prince Albert: He absolutely loves surprises, so it's a pity he's completely rubbish at keeping secrets. Despite a heavy German accent, while incognito he claims to hail from Glasgow. His cover isn't exactly deep, however: when asked about the Gorbals, he describes them as a lovely couple.

Queenie: She spent many a childhood Christmas wondering if her latest step-mother was going to lose her head. Chances were, if her father bought them a hat they'd keep it (the head that is . . . and the hat too).

Lord Melchett: He buys the Queen an expensive Christmas present. She's so grateful she'd consider marrying him if he wasn't as unattractive as a giant slug. Melchett is on the verge of becoming Duke of Kent and acquiring Windsor Castle, not to mention a saucy wife. He gets sentenced to death instead.

Nursie: The pronouncement of Lord Melchett's death sentence amuses her greatly.

George: Looking forward to spending Christmas with his friends Blackadder, Nelson and even Baldrick, he wonders what he can possibly do with a girl that he can't do in manly company. Blackadder can't conceive . . . Fortunately, the prince only has charades in mind. Blackadder attempts to explain the rules of the game to him for the umpteenth time. Upon hearing that the word 'Bible' has two syllables, George becomes confused: he remembers it having a fatted calf, but not two silly bulls, unless they were on Noah's Ark. He loves most things about Christmas of course, but not that depressing story about the chap born on Christmas Day who shoots his mouth off then comes a cropper in Johnny Arab Land. Yes, that Jesus really spoils the 'X-mas atmos'.

Name Checks: Mr Thicktwistle gives Blackadder a good deal on a Christmas twig from his Garden Emporium. Far from being malnourished, Tiny Tom is fifteen stone and built like a brick privy, with the likelihood of turning into a pie shop if he eats any more heartily. And as for his being a cripple: saying 'Phew, my leg hurts!' once in a while fools nobody except Baldrick. Due to the high infant mortality rate, a dog by the name of Spot is cast as the baby Jesus in the workhouse nativity play. Lady Jane Pottle was once a girl-friend of the Elizabethan Blackadder.

The World According to Ebenezer Blackadder: Upon hearing the tale of the stand-in baby Jesus, he is not convinced that 'Christianity would have established its firm grip over the hearts and minds of mankind if all Jesus ever said was "woof".'

Essential Information: According to Baldrick, it's spelt 'kweznuz'.

5: BLACKADDER
GOES FORTH

Over The Top

After filming *Blackadder the Third*, Rowan Atkinson told the *Radio Times* that he quite fancied playing the character next in the roaring twenties or as a member of the Royal Flying Corps during the First World War. For a while, rumours abounded that the former would indeed happen – however, such rumours had become commonplace by now and these were quite possibly based on nothing more than Atkinson's comment. There were also whispers of an 1890s setting, which would have allowed a welcome return for Miriam Margolyes' Queen Victoria. And some people thought that a Baron von Blackadder would fly into action for the Germans. In the end, this last group wasn't too far wrong: the next member of the Blackadder dynasty did indeed serve in the so-called War to End All Wars, albeit on the side of the English. And he did get to join the Royal Flying Corps, if only briefly.

The March of Time

Blackadder Goes Forth (the series cleverly avoiding any hint of consistency in the format of its numbering) took another leap through the years, into the twentieth century. However, Richard Curtis and Ben Elton confounded yet more early speculation that we would see a modern-day version of their characters. Instead, they took us to 1917 – the penultimate year of the First World War – to the Western Front and specifically to the dugout of one Captain Edmund Blackadder of the British Army.

By now, *Blackadder* was an established success story,

which meant, of course, that the BBC didn't have to increase
its budget one bit. As economical as ever, *Blackadder Goes
Forth* emulated its two immediate predecessors by playing
out important historical events at a very personal level and in,
for the most part, a couple of regular sets (although an aerial
dogfight is realised quite effectively with overdubbed stock
footage). Similarly, few privates are ever sighted in Blackadder's trench (oo-er, obviously).

If *Dad's Army* has always been an influence on Ben Elton,
then here's where it really starts to show, as the *Blackadder*
regulars clothe themselves in khaki and go off to fight for
king and country. One episode even features a Corporal
Jones, although the character as played by Stephen Frost
bears little resemblance to that created by Clive Dunn.

The Great War isn't just a backdrop, though; it also domi-
nates the storylines. Blackadder's feelings on the conflict and
on the men running it are made clear. As the series begins, he
has been in the trenches for several years and is dreading the
inevitable order to go over the top ('climbing over the top of
our trenches and walking slowly towards the enemy,' as he
puts it in the first episode, before noting that this tactic has
been tried before and 'everyone always gets slaughtered in
the first ten seconds'). Each of the six episodes revolves
around the captain's latest cunning plan to stave off that
fateful order or, better still, to get away from the front line
before it can arrive. He fakes a communications crisis, organ-
ises a show, becomes a war artist, a cook and a spy-catcher,
joins the Royal Flying Corps (as we've already mentioned)
and, finally and most memorably, fakes madness by sticking
two pencils up his nose (the script called for one pen but,
during rehearsal, it was decided that two would be funnier,
but another pen wasn't available, so pencils it had to be; thus
was a classic comedy moment created). In keeping with this
theme, the episodes were labelled 'Plan A' through to 'Plan
F' in publicity material, and therefore also in our guide. The
episode titles played up the wartime theme too, each going
for a double meaning based on military ranks – apart from
the last one, by which time they'd presumably run out of
them. The final episode is called, appropriately enough,

'Goodbyeee', although it is sometimes referred to (not least by Ben Elton) as the equally appropriate 'Over the Top'.

Playing Soldiers

As always, the latest Blackadder differed slightly from his ancestors. A moustache and an officer's uniform aided Atkinson in the creation of another unique character, albeit one that retains the cutting humour and world-weary cynicism that had become a trademark of all Blackadders after the original. Speaking to the *Radio Times*, he summed up the progression thus: 'In the first series, Blackadder was just an idiot. In the second series he was dashing but weak. As the butler, he became cleverer and nastier. This time he is less cruel and more careworn.' Our 'You Horrid Little Man' category is certainly a bit depleted this time around. Captain Blackadder doesn't mind whom he steps on in his quest to get out of the trenches, but that quest keeps him far too occupied to do any evil plotting beyond it. Unlike his ancestors (Ebenezer excepted, of course), he doesn't even kill anyone.

Also lost, more or less, is the character's anachronistic outlook. Obviously, with *Blackadder Goes Forth* being set only seventy-two years into the past – within the lifetimes of some of its viewers – it has a lot less to be 'Suspiciously Modern' about.

For the first time, Blackadder is completely removed from royalty. King George V doesn't appear at all, although he is mentioned in passing. It could be argued that, as the royal family became less powerful, successive Blackadders saw less point in sucking up to them. However, the fact that Captain Blackadder reports to the mad General Melchett rather than to a queen or a prince does make him seem weaker than his ancestors. So too does the fact that most of his plans must necessarily fail in order for the series' format to remain intact. Previous Blackadders had always imagined that they could influence the course of history – and some of them did. But this one is helpless to do anything of the sort, or even to control the course of his own life.

Blackadder is plagued by his own Baldrick, of course. As

the captain's faithful batman, it falls to him – in the absence of more than a few extras to appear around the trench from time to time – to represent all the working men that were conscripted into service during the war. He expresses their feelings at the conditions in which they are forced to live, their revolutionary stirrings at news that the Tsar of Russia has been overthrown and, of course, their fear of being sent over the top to die. Rowan Atkinson is often praised for his versatility in creating different Blackadders, but this is where Tony Robinson really shows that he's just as capable of doing likewise with the Baldrick family. Private S Baldrick (the 'S' having been adopted by an ancestor of his in 'Dish and Dishonesty') is every bit as odious and stupid as his predecessors, but Robinson gives him quite different mannerisms, notably a pronounced squint and a tendency to demonstrate his own stupidity quite loudly. It probably helped that the twentieth-century setting allowed the actor to wear his own glasses in the role for the first time (he has since had his sight corrected by laser treatment).

Blackadder is somewhat more indulgent of Baldrick than usual. Perhaps it is because, despite their differing ranks, they are in the same fix. Also, when Baldrick professes not to understand the causes of the war, or to see the reasoning behind Field Marshal Haig's latest strategy, it's not just because he's being thick.

Also back is Hugh Laurie's character, George, no longer of royal blood but still hailing from a privileged background (it had been intended that he should wear a monocle, to emphasise his image as an upper-class twit – but it kept falling out, so the idea was abandoned). George treats the war like a *Boy's Own* adventure and, initially at least, can't wait to leave the trenches and give the Germans a good seeing-to.

Despite its superficial differences, the structure of *Blackadder Goes Forth* isn't far removed from that of its predecessors, and *Blackadder II* in particular. George may be descended from a prince, but here he is reinvented as a more than adequate replacement for the long-lost Percy. The Blackadder/Baldrick/George trio is established in one location, with Blackadder frequently travelling to a second to meet with a mad superior who has the power of life and death over him. That superior is a descendant of *Blackadder II*'s Melchett, albeit one that has little in common with the refined, religious lord of Elizabethan times. Stephen Fry's General Anthony Cecil Hogmanay Melchett has more in common with the same actor's Duke of Wellington, seen in 'Duel and Duality', being as he is a raving nutter who comes complete with the trademark bellow ('Baaaaa!') that Fry puts down to 'smoking asthma'.

If General Melchett is little like Lord Melchett, then Captain Darling is nothing at all like Lord Percy, despite being played by Tim McInnerny. Back in a regular role, McInnerny's wish not to play the character that made him a famous idiot was still in force. Instead, as Melchett's sneering, officious, toadying aide-de-camp, he fulfils a function that *Blackadder the Third* did without: that of the ineffectual assistant to the authority figure (i.e., the original Melchett's role).

So, to summarise, *Blackadder Goes Forth* is a bit like *Blackadder II*, except that Hugh Laurie plays Tim McInnerny's role, McInnerny plays Stephen Fry's role, Fry plays Miranda Richardson's role and, just to complete the set, Richardson sort of plays Laurie's role in that she just turns up as a guest star again. As 'General Hospital's' Nurse Mary Fletcher-Brown, she creates a character similar to 'Amy and Amiability's' Amy: all wet and fluffy at first, but with a hidden aspect to her personality.

In a series that is otherwise quite short on guest appearances, both Rik Mayall and Gabrielle Glaister strengthen the link to *Blackadder II* by reprising their roles as Lord Flashheart and 'Bob' respectively (the latter in two episodes), both first and last seen in 'Bells'.

On Parade

The opening and closing titles of the series were specially filmed at the army barracks at Colchester, with the latter being shown in black and white and treated to look as if they might really be seven decades old. The 3rd Battalion of the Royal Anglian Regiment (alias the Pompadours, according to the credits) were on hand to provide a literal army of extras and to perform a very military version of the familiar *Blackadder* theme, arranged of course by Howard Goodall and led by bandmaster Tim Parkinson.

Originally, Fry and McInnerny were to have taken the troops' salute on horseback. However, as Fry explained during an on-line chat with the AOL *Black Adder* club, 'I was given the colonel's horse – about four hundred hands high, jet black and severely ungelded. His name was Thunderbolt, which should have warned me. He was fine at first, but as soon as the band started up . . . he shied like a startled mustang and threatened to unseat me. Hugh and Rowan laughed so much at my discomfiture that the filming proved impossible.' The pair stood on a podium instead.

Standing Orders

The edition of *Radio Times* for the week in which *Blackadder Goes Forth* was first transmitted contains an illuminating feature on the series. Richard Curtis himself provided the magazine with condensed 'military service histories' for each of the major characters, and also a few extracts from Blackadder's diary. Between them, these documents reveal some details that might otherwise never have seen the light of day.

Captain Blackadder, we learn, joined the army for an easy life of 'sitting in armchairs and ordering drinks across three continents'. His heroism at Mboto Gorge is mentioned (see 'Goodbyeee') but the outbreak of war was, presumably, a bit of a bugger for him, given his resolution to avoid facing enemies who actually possessed guns.

Arriving at the front in September 1914, Blackadder was introduced to General Hogmanay Melchett and Captain Darling. 'To describe him as mad as a hatter,' he commented on the former, 'would be to cast an unforgiveable slur upon the mental state of hatters all over the world.' Melchett – whose cousin, apparently, sent the Light Brigade off on their ill-fated charge – was a member of Oundle's great fag-beating team in 1877, going on to break wind for his college at Oxford. His reasons for joining the army were twofold: 'to protect the British Empire and shout at the lower classes in a very loud voice.'

Darling joined up in 1904, swiftly climbed the ranks to became a captain four years later, then became Melchett's aide-de-camp and climbed no further. Frequently the butt of the general's insults, he clings to the hope that his senior officer is just joking.

Resolving to see as little of Melchett and Darling as possible, Blackadder looked forward to the arrival of his 'truly remarkable young batman', Private Baldrick. By October 1914, he had revised his opinion. 'All I can say, to his credit, is that since this is the very worst, ugliest, and vilest place on God's earth, he is at least the right man in the right place at the right time.' Baldrick, possessor of the shortest haircut in the armed forces, graduated from the Turnip Street Workhouse, where he majored in gutter-sweeping and potato-peeling. It is noted that his Christian name is 'uncertain'. Foreshadowing the episode 'Captain Cook', Blackadder also comments upon Baldrick's lack of culinary skills, which, one night in October, stretched to rat stroganoff. Still, he could console himself with the knowledge that he was about to be joined by 'a splendid young lieutenant.'

Within two months, Blackadder was referring to said lieutenant – George St Barleigh as he is named here – as George Blancmange-for-Brains. Blaming his mental state upon interbreeding, he remarked that 'if English aristocratic families don't soon stop making a point of pointing their members at other members of the family, all will be lost.' George, conversely, numbered his 'splendidly courageous leader' Blackadder amongst his heroes, along with General Melchett and Lawrence of Arabia. Having won the Boy Most Unlikely to String Together an Intelligent Sentence Cup at a major public school, he joined the army on the first day of the war, 'dying for a good scrap'. We are also told that he used yellow wart ointment, at least until it disappeared – along with Blackadder's shaving cream – on the day that Baldrick made lemon meringue pie.

After two years in such company, Blackadder claimed that he could no longer remember what he was fighting for. 'I'm now fighting,' he commented in December 1916, 'for the right not to spend any more time with General Melchett, Captain Darling, Lieutenant George and Private Baldrick. Surely that's not too much to ask?'

Reports from the Front Line

'Rowan Atkinson and co.'s finest yet,' said Hilary Kingsley in the *Mirror*.

'Wherever he finds himself,' said Peter Tory of the *Daily Express*, 'Atkinson remains one of the most hilarious men on the telly.'

Yep, the praise of *Blackadder Goes Forth* was, for the first time, pretty unanimous. Was the series really so much better than its predecessors? Or might we be cynical enough to suspect that *Blackadder* had, by now, passed beyond criticism? Certainly, it had become one of the UK's most loved programmes – *Blackadder Goes Forth* carried off a BAFTA award for Best Light Entertainment Series, just as *Blackadder the Third* had before it – and it would have taken a brave critic to go against the tide of opinion.

Writing in the *Guardian*, Hugh Herbert did dare to make a few contrary points, even if his conclusion was that *Blackadder Goes Forth* was 'emetic but unmissable'. 'If Edmund Blackadder now seems more weary than wittily vicious,' he opined, 'that's because the more convoluted conceits of the Richard Curtis/Ben Elton scripts sound right in doublet and hose but sound strained in khaki.' Perhaps surprisingly, Herbert considered 'the suggestion that this fourth series has a more satirical purpose is pure smokescreen,' noting that the *Blackadder* formula remained unchanged: 'dunderheads in charge, elegant blackguard on the make and, tripping over his own cleverness, Baldrick face down in the mud.' Er . . . surely he didn't mean to say that Baldrick tripped over his own cleverness? Perhaps that comma before 'tripping' shouldn't be there?

Of course, when Herbert wrote that review, *Blackadder Goes Forth* had yet to make its own most powerful point. Curiously, the critics themselves were all but silent on the subject of the series' final episode, 'Goodbyeee', and the scene that everyone else was talking about.

'It certainly touched the teenagers in the school where I teach,' wrote a *Radio Times* reader from Livingston, West Lothian. 'Many of them were stunned at the sad ending to the characters with whom they empathised. This comedy, more than any serious programme they had watched on the Great War, affected them deeply. It was a great moment in television history.' The same reader commented that 'the impact on young people in "Poppy Week" can only be guessed at.' The writer of this congratulatory missive? A Mr John Lloyd. Surely some mistake?

'When the series was first announced, I was dubious about the Great War being a suitable case for the *Blackadder* treatment,' wrote Shirley Collins of Brighton, who was apparently left in tears by the series' conclusion. 'I should have known that the *Blackadder* team was to be utterly trusted. They shone a clear light on those who were culpable and on the horror and futility of it all, while still making it a truly comic series . . . That final scene will stay with me a long time.'

However, Julia Wolfe-Harlow of Loughton, Essex, wasn't happy about 'the way in which *Blackadder Goes Forth* has made fun of the First World War.' She recounted the tale of how her 'gentleman', Harry, died in 1916, 'together with thousands of others, in a charge ordered by General Haig', adding that he 'paid for this country's mistakes with his life.'

Upsetting though it may have been for Ms Wolfe-Harlow, though, that was exactly the point that 'Goodbyeee' made.

That Final Scene

It was almost by accident that *Blackadder II* and *Blackadder the Third* had followed the example of *The Black Adder* by killing off the central character in the final episode (OK, so *Blackadder the Third* only killed off his name . . .). However, the final scene of *Blackadder Goes Forth* was one of the first things on which the writers decided. 'We were very keen to do World War I,' Richard Curtis told the BBC's *Laughter in the House: The Story of British Sitcom* in 1999, 'but it's recent history – and terrible and tragic recent history. So, our deal with ourselves was that we would do it as long as we would kill all the characters.'

'Goodbyeee' is certainly uncompromising. After six episodes of jokes about the futility of war, the madness of such men as General Melchett and the consequences of that madness for those unfortunate enough to be living or dying at their whim, the truth behind the comedy is driven home with force. Blackadder faces what he has striven to avoid. He is ordered to go over the top; to make what will certainly be a suicidal run against the enemy in the hope of gaining a little extra ground.

'Goodbyeee' is short on storyline, but it provides a lot of background to the characters. Their hopes and aspirations are laid bare. We learn why each of them joined the army, and are told that both Baldrick and George have lost all their friends to the war (none of Baldrick's friends were human, but all the same . . .). Even George is now frightened of losing his life for nothing. When viewed with foreknowledge of their fate, it all seems very poignant indeed. Of particular note is Tim McInnerny's tear-jerking performance as Darling, who is devastated to find himself reassigned to the front line. When the order comes for the big push, only Melchett is conspicuous by his absence.

Not that the episode is humourless; far from it. Richard Curtis has commented that, by this time, he had learned that it was possible to go from comedy to drama in an instant. It's an effective technique. Blackadder keeps that famed British stiff upper lip, and cracks jokes up until the penultimate line of the series. On a first viewing, this lulls the viewer into expecting a last-minute reprieve, so it is all the more shocking when no such reprieve arrives.

Baldrick's final cunning plan isn't even heard. As the signal is given, Blackadder simply wishes his troops good luck, signalling that the time for jokes is over.

As Blackadder, Baldrick, George and Darling charge to their deaths, the action is slowed down and the picture fades to a simple image of a field of poppies. The credits and closing theme of the episode are omitted. Logos for both

Blackadder and the BBC appear along with the date in the bottom left-hand corner of the screen, to emphasise that this *is* the end – but the final image of the series is that field. It is arguably one of the most powerful and poignant images ever seen on television, and it would linger in viewers' minds for a long time to come.

Ten years later, a poll conducted by Channel 4 and the *Observer* newspaper to discern the top 100 most memorable TV moments of all time found that final scene notching up a very impressive ninth place. Every other entry in the top ten – apart from number seven, which was Delboy from *Only Fools and Horses* falling through a bar – was a news report of a major event (number one was the 1969 moon landing).

'We didn't plan to make the ending moving . . . but we did plan to make it sincere,' Ben Elton said in 1999, when the BBC produced a *Best of British* special devoted to his work.

In the same programme, Hugh Laurie indirectly addressed Hugh Herbert's points: 'One of the reasons it was so effective is that actually the characters and the attitude was very similar [to previous series], it's just that the context was so massively different. It startled people.' And he's right, you know. *Blackadder Goes Forth* may just have been another reworking of an established formula – but it's precisely because it dealt, as Richard Curtis said, with more recent and tragic history that, this time, that formula conveyed an unforgettable message.

Blackadder Goes Forth

Captain Edmund Blackadder (Rowan Atkinson)
Private S Baldrick (Tony Robinson)
General Sir Anthony Cecil Hogmanay Melchett
(Stephen Fry)
Lieutenant The Honourable George Colthurst St Barleigh
(Hugh Laurie)
Captain Kevin Darling (Tim McInnerny)

Written by Richard Curtis and Ben Elton;
directed by Richard Boden; produced by John Lloyd.

PLAN A: CAPTAIN COOK

First Broadcast: 28 September 1989.

Blackadder is suspicious when a new revolver and trench-climbing ladders arrive. Fearing that it's time to go over the top, he almost considers Baldrick's plan of escaping the trenches by becoming a cook at Staff HQ. Then an opening presents itself for an artist to leave the front line and produce a stirring cover for *King and Country* magazine. George turns out to be surprisingly good, so Blackadder and Baldrick pose as a noble Tommy and a murdered nun respectively while he paints them. Blackadder, of course, takes the credit, and is appointed official war artist. Unfortunately, the *King and Country* story was a bluff. Blackadder is sent into No Man's Land to produce accurate drawings of enemy positions. After an unsuccessful sortie into a minefield, though, he has a better idea. George produces a fake picture, which shows the Germans so well prepared that the push will have to be cancelled. Except that that's just what they'll be expecting . . . Looks like it's back to Plan A, then. Blackadder, George and Baldrick miss the big push by hiding out in Staff HQ, disguised as wandering Italian chefs and serving up Baldrick's unique cuisine.

Cunning Plans: Baldrick carves his name on to a bullet: after all, if he owns the bullet with his name on it, then he can't be killed by it. His cunning plan to avoid fighting by becoming a cook is almost the first brilliant plan that a Baldrick has ever had – 'For centuries we've tried, and they've always turned out to be total pigswill' – except that he's no good at cooking. Field Marshal Haig has a brilliant plan, too: it involves his men getting out of their trenches and walking slowly towards the enemy. They certainly won't expect that, given that it's been tried eighteen times already and tends to lead to the slaughter of British forces.

Cutting Comments: Blackadder tells Baldrick that, if a cannibal cracked his head open, there wouldn't be enough water in there to cover a small water biscuit (because his brain's so small, you see) – and that a wimple suits him, because it covers his face. He idly wonders if Melchett has ever visited Earth.

You Horrid Little Man: Nothing too horrid at all, really. Blackadder takes credit for George's painting, and he threatens Baldrick with a broken nose. But that's about it.

Double Entendres: Missing Blackadder's implication that *King and Country* is useful only as toilet paper, Melchett comments: 'I thought it would be right up your alley.' Posing as a nun, Baldrick says he wants a wimple – but he should have gone before they started. George suggests that Blackadder should pose naked, citing artistic licence and the willing suspension of disbelief. 'I'm not having anyone staring in disbelief at my willy suspension!' he retorts.

Tortuous Similes: *King and Country* is 'about as convincing as Doctor Crippen's defence lawyer'. Blackadder's men have 'the artistic talent of a cluster of colour-blind hedgehogs – in a bag.' George considers himself and Baldrick 'the stupidest stupids in the history of stupiditiness.'

Blackadder: He smokes a pipe. Though lacking George's public school education, he considers himself a fully rounded human being with a degree from the University of Life. He never paid attention in nursery art classes, as he was too busy frightening one Sarah Wallis by making huge willies out of papier mâché. He likes to keep an informal trench, but only when it suits him. He considers carving his own headstone with the epitaph 'Here lies Edmund Blackadder, and he's bloody annoyed.'

Baldrick: He and the other men are desperate for solid fuel, having burnt both the trench-climbing ladders and the cat. His mother is still alive and less good-looking than Punch. He is the worst cook in the world, though that's mainly down to his choice of ingredients. His filets mignons in sauce béarnaise don't taste like dog turds in glue for no reason, you know. Advised by George to paint whatever comes from within, he vomits on to his easel. His father was taken to court more than once; when asked his occupation he always said what, to Baldrick's ears, sounded like 'nun'. The idea of the big push terrifies Baldrick.

George: Education wasn't a priority at his school; all a boy had to learn was how to 'hit a six, sing the school song very loud and take a hot crumpet from behind without blubbing.' The only thing he's ever been good at is painting. He is known to Melchett through his family connections (his Uncle Bertie) and university background (he studied at Cambridge), and is thus granted a week's leave to attend the boat race. He obeys his senior officers unquestioningly, even when Blackadder orders him to remain silent while he takes credit for George's work in front of him. Though well aware of his own stupidity, he lets his imagination run riot on his picture of enemy positions and includes a few more elephants than he ought to have done. He eagerly awaits the push and is dismayed when it seems that it might be cancelled. When it isn't, he feels compelled to shout 'Bravo!' at an annoyingly loud volume, although, of course, he seeks permission first.

Melchett: He used to break wind for his college and he enthuses that the push will result in 'the greatest victory since the Winchester flower-arranging team beat Harrow by twelve sore bottoms to one.' He wishes he could be out dodging bullets with Blackadder and his men, instead of dining on fine food at Staff HQ. Or so he says.

Darling: He doesn't like being called Darling by Blackadder, presumably because of the way he says it. He copies Melchett's mannerisms and sometimes moves his lips in time with the general's. Despite this, Melchett considers him 'a pen-pushing, desk-sucking blotter-jotter'. He's suspicious of Blackadder and annoyed to hear him criticise his superiors, but too weak to do anything about it.

Name Checks: Corporal Black is Melchett's hairdresser, whom the mad general twice confuses with Blackadder. Having bumped into a chap called Bernard in the mess the other day, Melchett added him to the list of people allowed to know official secrets, along with Field Marshal Haig, Haig's wife and all of Haig's wife's friends. Sarah Wallis was an easily frightened nursery school contemporary of Blackadder. George's Uncle Bertie was one of Melchett's fellow wind-breakers.

The War According to Captain Blackadder: He describes *King and Country* as 'the greatest work of fiction since vows of fidelity were included in the French marriage service.' What George thinks of as giving the Hun a good thrashing is, to Blackadder, 'yet another gargantuan effort to move his [Field Marshal Haig's] drinks cabinet six inches closer to Berlin.' Upon learning that Haig wants to cheer his men up, he suggests his resignation and suicide. When Melchett assures Baldrick that he and Darling will be right behind him in the big push, Blackadder's estimate is about thirty-five miles behind.

Essential Knowledge: To sauté a rat, you shave it and marinate it in a puddle until it's drowned, then stretch it out under a hot light bulb. To fricassee it, you do exactly the same but with a bigger rat.

PLAN B: CORPORAL PUNISHMENT

First Broadcast: 5 October 1989.

Corporal Perkins (Jeremy Hardy)
Corporal Jones (Stephen Frost)
Private Fraser (Lee Cornes)
Private Robinson (Paul Mark Elliott)
Private Tipplewick (Jeremy Gittins)

Blackadder fakes a series of telephone malfunctions to explain why Melchett's orders to go over the top haven't been received. He also shoots a carrier pigeon, only to learn that the shooting of pigeons has become a court martial offence. When both George and Baldrick deny having eaten General Melchett's beloved, delicious, plump-breasted Speckled Jim, suspicions are aroused. Imprisoned, Blackadder sends out two notes, which Baldrick duly mixes up. Blackadder receives a spongebag from England's finest lawyer and is represented in court by George. Worse still, Melchett has appointed himself judge in the trial of the Flanders Pigeon Murderer, and he's already asking for his black cap. Awaiting execution at dawn by a more-than-usually-jocular firing squad, Blackadder learns that George's Uncle Rupert is the Minister of War. George only has to send a telegram and a reprieve will be granted. Alas, George and Baldrick celebrate too soon. Waking with hangovers, they realise that the all-important telegram was never despatched. They're a bit surprised, then, to find Blackadder alive, Uncle Rupert having stepped in of his own volition upon hearing how Melchett conducted the court martial. And, when an opportunity arises for two volunteers to participate in Operation: Certain Death, Blackadder has just the men.

Watch Out For: Lee Cornes, last seen in 'Ink and Incapability', makes his third *Blackadder* appearance. Stephen

Frost, last seen as long ago as 'Witchsmeller Pursuivant', makes his second. Jeremy Hardy is now best known as a presenter and for his appearances on radio and TV panel shows, notably BBC 2's *If I Ruled the World*. Paul Mark Elliott appeared in *Press Gang* and was a regular in *Joking Apart*, which, along with *Blackadder*, would make any actor's CV complete.

Cunning Plans: Baldrick smuggles an escape kit into prison, but it consists of a wooden duck (for balancing on top of the head, as a brilliant disguise if caught near water), a pencil (to drop Baldrick a line to say how the escape went) and a miniature trumpet (for winning the favour of a difficult child, should it prove necessary). No saws, hammers, chisels, guns or false passports at all, then – although there is a change of clothes, in the form of a Robin Hood costume.

Cutting Comments: Blackadder hopes that Darling's mother will die in a freak yachting accident. 'I know you mean to be friendly,' he says to his chirpy firing squad, 'but I hope you won't take it amiss if I ask you to sod off and die!'

You Horrid Little Man: Blackadder kills a pigeon. The rotter!

Double Entendres: George longs to give the Nazis a taste of British spunk. Darling phones Blackadder, comments on the terrible line at his end and tells him he's to advance on the enemy at once – which, according to Blackadder, sounds like 'he's got a terrible lion up his end so there's an advantage to an enema at once.' Baldrick's attempt to say 'gobbledegook' comes out as 'gobble a Duke'. George's Uncle Rupert can 'pull strings, scratch backs, fiddle with knobs . . .' Blackadder's jailer, Perkins, has to admire his prisoner's balls – 'Perhaps later,' says Blackadder.

Tortuous Similes: Blackadder wants his case to be 'as watertight as a mermaid's brassiere', which might prove difficult as he's 'as guilty as a puppy sitting beside a pile of poo.' Baldrick concludes that Blackadder is 'as dead as some doodoos,' while George considers himself 'as thick as the big print version of *The Complete Works of Charles Dickens*.'

Blackadder: He's an excellent shot. He is calm in the face of death: when Melchett tells him he's to die at dawn, Blackadder asks for an alarm call. He's not a religious man but, upon learning that George and Baldrick almost caused his death, he swears to 'pray nightly to the God who killed Cain and squashed Samson that he comes out of retirement and gets back into practice with the pair of you.'

Baldrick: Advised to deny everything in court, he denies that his name is Baldrick, that he's Blackadder's batman and that George is George. He helps George to think by hitting him with a cricket bat. It works, sort of, as it actually jars Baldrick's memory.

George: His uncle's a lawyer, but he's not. In fact, his School Debating Society voted him Boy Least Likely to Complete a Coherent Sentence (well, that's what we assume, as he doesn't quite finish telling us). He hopes to play the 'mindless optimism card' strongly during the trial, but he's a little too eager to tell the truth in court. His mother (whom he calls Mumsie) sends him cases of Scotch. He has a little cousin called Freddy, who plays cricket, and another relative called Celia, who enters pony club trials. His Mad Uncle Rupert has recently become the Minister of War. When George was initiated into the Silly Buggers Society at Cambridge, he misheard the rules and tried to push an aubergine up his earhole.

Melchett: He likes the word 'gobbledegook', and tells Darling to make a note of it for use in future conversations. His pigeon had been with him since he was a child; he hand-reared it from a chick and it was his true love and his only childhood friend. He doesn't care that Blackadder has disobeyed orders – he wouldn't even care if he'd been 'rogering the Duke of York with a prize-winning leek' – he's only concerned with Speckled Jim's fate, which prompts him to attack Blackadder with his swagger stick. Persuaded to do things by the book, Melchett nevertheless ensures that Blackadder's trial can have only one outcome. He acts as both chief prosecution witness and judge, switching effortlessly from the angry outburst of the former to the detached air of the latter.

Darling: As soon as Melchett turns against Blackadder, he is free to list his own suspicions. He is a calming influence upon the enraged general. Blackadder taunts him by suggesting that he's a dogsbody – but, in fact, he appears for the prosecution in court and intends to have a lot of fun. He's been keeping a diary of all the times that Blackadder has disobeyed orders – to the minute.

Name Checks: A telegram arrives, ordering a Catpain Blackudder to go over the top; Blackadder bins it, having never heard of the chap. He hopes to engage Bob Massingbird as his lawyer, as he has the finest mind in English legal history. In the Case of the Bloody Knife, Massingbird was able to get a man acquitted of murder and knighted despite thirteen witnesses and a confession. He also successfully prosecuted 'big, bearded, bonking, butch' Oscar Wilde, father of one hundred and fourteen illegitimate children and author of *Why I Like to Do It With Girls*, for homosexuality. George's Uncle Rupert intervenes to save Blackadder's life when he hears how 'that arse Melchett' conducted himself during the court martial.

Essential Knowledge: The penalty for disobeying orders is not, in fact, court martial followed by immediate cessation of chocolate rations. It's court martial followed by immediate death by firing squad. So, Blackadder was only half right.

PLAN C: MAJOR STAR

First Broadcast: 12 October 1989.

Driver Parkhurst (Gabrielle Glaister)

Revolution is in the air, and Melchett wants a concert party to boost his men's morale. Seeing his ticket out of the trenches, Blackadder worms his way into the job of organiser. The general assigns his driver, Bob Parkhurst, to help him, unaware that Bob is, of course, a girl. Baldrick unveils his Charlie Chaplin impression, prompting Blackadder to write to Mr

Chaplin with news that he's found the only person in the world less funny than he is. George becomes Gorgeous Georgina and the show, despite being awful, is a hit. If the second night plays as well, then it's off to the London Palladium. But first, Melchett wants a date . . . with Georgina. Forced to oblige, George gets carried away – and, indeed, engaged – forcing Blackadder to pretend that Georgina has accidentally danced on to a cluster of mines and been killed. Without a leading lady, the renamed Georgina Melchett Memorial Show is in jeopardy. Bob steps in, but Melchett is revolted at the sight of his driver in a dress, and the show is cancelled. It's no longer necessary, anyway, as the Americans have joined the war, bringing with them the world's biggest collection of morale-boosting Charlie Chaplin films. And Chaplin himself wants Blackadder to be the projectionist.

Cunning Plans: Baldrick presents his latest cunning plan, which is to replace Georgina – not on stage but as Melchett's wife. This is, of course, the worst plan since Abraham Lincoln decided to take in a show.

Cutting Comments: Blackadder admires Charlie Chaplin's genius in inventing 'a way of getting paid a million dollars a year for wearing a pair of stupid trousers.' On Baldrick's performance, he remarks that 'in the Amazonian rainforests, there are tribes of Indians as yet untouched by civilisation who have developed more convincing Charlie Chaplin impressions than yours.' George, he thinks, is 'the least convincing female impressionist since Tarzan went through Jane's handbag and ate her lipstick.'

You Horrid Little Man: Blackadder kicks Baldrick up the backside twice, just to prove that it isn't funny. 'If I should die,' he tells George, 'think only this of me: I'll be back to get you!' He takes out his frustrations on Darling by offering him a liquorice allsort – which, of course, is Baldrick's slug.

Double Entendres: The Russian masses have risen up and shot their nobs, and the top echelons of the French army have suffered horrendous uprisings from the bottom. Blackadder has a good line in rough shag, and will be more than happy to fill Bob's pipe. Melchett expects that Georgina has more spunk than most women.

Tortuous Similes: Blackadder is beyond being cheesed off. He's moved on to coffee and cigars 'and at this late stage I am in a cab with two lady companions on my way to the Pink Pussycat in Lower Regent Street.' He finds Chaplin's films 'about as funny as getting an arrow through the neck and then discovering there's a gas bill tied to it.' Baldrick thinks they're 'as funny as a vegetable that has grown into a rude and amusing shape,' which, to Blackadder's mind, is a whole-hearted agreement. He puts it to Bob that she's 'a girl with as much talent for disguise as a giraffe in dark glasses trying to get into a polar bears only golf club.' George needs applause 'in the same way that an ostler needs his ostle.' The loss of Georgina puts Blackadder in 'the stickiest situation since Sticky the stick insect got stuck on a sticky bun.'

Blackadder: When the Russians pull out of the war, it's the last straw for him. Believing that the entire German army will use his nipples for target practice, he intends to desert – until Melchett reminds him what happens to deserters. Blackadder would rather stand on a stepladder in No Man's Land, 'smoking endless cigarettes through a luminous balaclava', than organise a concert party – until a move out of the trenches is mooted. He's obviously more astute than his Elizabethan ancestor, as he sees through Bob's disguise immediately.

Baldrick: He stands up to Blackadder for the first time, events in Russia having convinced him that it's time to throw off 'hated oppressors like you and the lieutenant . . . present company excepted, sir.' Of course, he goes straight off to clean the latrines when ordered. His Chaplin impression consists of wearing a hat and balancing a dead slug on his top lip. He seizes (what he thinks is) his chance to marry Melchett. He hasn't turned his back on his revolutionary principles, though: he intends to bring the aristocracy down from within, like a sort of 'frozen horse'. He sleeps in a puddle.

George: He's a big fan of Charlie Chaplin. Blackadder thinks he'd do well as a limbo dancer, as everything goes over his head. He loves the theatre – it's in his blood – and, unlike Bob, he doesn't know when to get off. Women's clothing makes him feel fantastic. He is self-deprecating about his performance to the point of insisting that he was awful – but when Blackadder agrees with him, he blubs. He's appalled at the idea of dating Melchett but is soon carried away by the romance. He accepts the general's proposal because, after all, he's a senior officer. Melchett calls him Chipmunk, because his nose is just like a Chipmunk's.

Melchett: He shoots deserters as a matter of course and considers that anyone who wants to sit out the war would have to be a damp-eyed nancy-boy. He is blind to both Bob's femininity and Georgina's lack of it. He fears that Georgina will find him too old and crusty, though a bushy moustache should help him catch her. His idea of seductive technique is to cover his date with pepper and sneeze all over her. He's not married, having waited all his life for the perfect woman in whose ear to dribble. He asks Blackadder to be his best man. Hearing that there's something wrong with Georgina, the worst he can imagine is that she's Welsh. He demonstrates his changeable emotions again, recovering from his loss of Georgina in an instant.

Darling: Regimental business forces him to miss the first show: there's a delivery of paperclips.

Name Checks: Corporals Smith and Johnson appear as The Three Silly Twerps (the joke being that there's only two). George suggests suitable transvestites – all presumably from Blackadder's trench – for the second show, but Corporal Cartwright looks like an orang-utan, Willis is too short, Petheridge is too old and Taplow is too dead. The slug gets a name: it's called Graham.

The War According to Captain Blackadder: If Bob wanted to see how a war was fought so badly, then she's come to the right place: 'A war hasn't been fought this badly since Olaf the Hairy, High Chief of All the Vikings, accidentally ordered eighty thousand battle helmets with the horns on the inside.'

Essential Knowledge: The troops hear news that Tsar Nicholas II of Russia has been overthrown; therefore, this episode must begin shortly after 15 March 1917. The concert party, then, must take longer to organise than Melchett implies it will, as the Americans entered the war – late as usual – on 6 April.

PLAN D: PRIVATE PLANE

First Broadcast: 19 October 1989.

Squadron Commander Lord Flashheart (Rik Mayall)
Baron Von Richthoven (sic) (Adrian Edmondson)
Lieutenant Von Gerhardt (Hugo E Blick)
Driver Parkhurst (Gabrielle Glaister)

When Squadron Commander the Lord Flashheart is downed in Blackadder's trench, the captain is unimpressed. Realising, however, that the Royal Flying Corps could be a cushy number, he applies to join. There are only two problems. One: his instructor is Flashheart. Two: George was wrong; they aren't called the Twenty Minuters for the amount of time they spend in their planes, it's their average life expectancy. Blackadder takes to the air with Baldrick as his navigator, but a brief encounter with the Red Baron Von Richthoven persuades him to crash land. Alas, it seems the Germans advanced a mile last night, which puts him on the wrong side of the lines (although seventeen square feet of land have been recaptured, which is something). Blackadder expects to be rogered to death, but Von Richthoven intends to humiliate his proud adversary by having him teach home economics to young girls at a convent school outside Heidelberg. So, the captain's a bit miffed when George and Flashheart come to his rescue. Von Richthoven and Flashheart face each other for the first time as natural enemies, men of honour . . . till Flashheart shoots the Kraut dead in mid-soliloquy, frees his prisoners, knocks out Darling and runs off with Bob. Woof, woof!

Watch Out For: Rik Mayall brings along his long-time partner in comedy (*The Comic Strip Presents, The Young Ones, Filthy, Rich and Catflap, Bottom*, etc.) Adrian Edmondson.

Cutting Comments: Blackadder doesn't want to have to write to Baldrick's mother at London Zoo with news of the death of 'her only human child'. When Baldrick wishes he could fly up where the air is clear, Blackadder points out that the air will never be clear around him. Not recognising Baldrick's aeroplane impression, he explains: 'I always get confused between the sound of a Sopwith Camel and the sound of a malodorous runt wasting everyone's time.' He is less impressed by Flashheart than by the contents of his handkerchief. When Baldrick wants his mum, Blackadder agrees that 'a maternally outraged gorilla' might come in handy. Flashheart calls Baldrick 'the mound of the Hound of the Baskervilles'.

You Horrid Little Man: George turns up to rescue an unwilling Blackadder, and gets a cell door in his face.

Double Entendres: Flashheart doesn't want five hundred girls on his conscience, just on his face. He runs out of juice but, fortunately for said girls, he means petrol. Bob hangs around with big nobs, so she should be used to a fellow like Flash, who threatens to give an unco-operative official's wife something to hang her towels on. He likes girls direct and to his point and is in favour of the Suffragette Movement as 'any bird who wants to chain herself to my railing and *suffer a jet movement* gets my vote', etc., etc.

Suspiciously Modern: A-ha! An anachronistic reference at last, as Flashheart reminisces about a daring flight through a woman's bedroom window with a box of chocolates. You know, like in the famous Milk Tray TV advert. Of course, the Milk Tray man didn't then shoot off and shag the woman's sister.

Tortuous Similes: Flashheart finds Bob 'saucier than a direct hit on a Heinz factory' and boasts that the RFC offers 'a uniform so smart it's got a PhD from Cambridge.' Blackadder is peeved at landing behind enemy lines, as 'for two and a half years the Western Front's been as likely to move as a Frenchman who lives next door to a brothel.' Facing death, he 'couldn't be more petrified if a wild rhinoceros had just come home from a hard day at the swamp and found me wearing his pyjamas, smoking his cigars and in bed with his wife.'

Blackadder: He claims that, as a boy, he watched marsh warblers swooping in his mother's undercroft – but he might be lying. He doesn't like being called Captain Slackbladder. He'll happily sacrifice his pride in return for his life.

Baldrick: He worships Flashheart and, upon meeting him, wishes he could write so that he could send a letter home about 'this golden moment'. His entire family took up smoking so they could get every cigarette card ever printed of the air ace. They succeeded and, thanks to the valiant sacrifice of Baldrick's grandmother, they got the album, too. Baldrick doesn't know his arse from his elbow – literally. His stomach goes all squirty when he's afraid, and he's an expert at breaking wind.

George: He's not entirely confident about being able to count to one hundred, although five should be all right. He possesses a Brooke Bond *Book of the Air* (missing a few stickers). He considers Blackadder a friend and, surprisingly, is prepared to defy Darling to help him. He had a pet rabbit, Flossy, which was cruelly killed in a variety of ways on his sixth birthday; George blubbed when he was given a slice of rabbit pie instead of birthday cake.

Melchett: He's always sensed a touch of 'battle-dodging, nappy-wearing "I'd rather have a cup of tea than charge stark naked at Jerry" ' about the men in the trenches, but those of the Twenty Minuters have his full admiration and are welcome to marry his sister (he wants her out of the house anyway, as she makes an awful noise when eating boiled egg). While visiting George's family, he once set his dog on George's pet rabbit, after which the kindest thing to do was run over it in his car. When that didn't work, he shot it. He's stark raving mad.

Darling: He was refused a transfer to the Women's Auxiliary Balloon Corps. One of his important responsibilities is to dust the office. He considers that a mission to rescue Blackadder would be an unreasonable use of time and resources.

Name Checks: The Royal Flying Corps is headed by Air Chief Marshal Sir Hugh Massingbird-Massingbird, VC DFC and bar (a relation of Bob Massingbird from 'Corporal Punishment'?). Blackadder claims that Flashheart is less popular than Wee Jock Poo-Pong McPlop, who cleans the public toilets in Aberdeen.

The War According to Captain Blackadder: He sees no point in shelling the Germans as the net effect so far has been 'one dachshund with a slight limp'. Flashheart and his Flying Aces are the biggest show-offs since Lady Godiva ('I don't care how many times they go up-diddly-up-up, they're still gits.') and, what's more, they're a bunch of upper-class delinquents who loaf about in Paris drinking champagne and enjoying 'moist, pink, highly experienced French peasant girls'. Which is what persuades him to apply. He considers the Germans' reputation for brutality justified by their interminable operas and their lack of a word for 'fluffy'. Their nation 'consists almost entirely of very fat men in leather shorts burping to the tune of "She'll Be Coming Round the Mountain".' The war would have been simpler if the army had just stayed in England and shot fifty thousand of their own men each week.

Essential Knowledge: Some sound advice from Melchett to George, when Blackadder and Baldrick are missing: 'If nothing else works, a total pig-headed unwillingness to look facts in the face will see us through.'

PLAN E: GENERAL HOSPITAL

First Broadcast: 26 October 1989.

Nurse Mary (Miranda Richardson)
Brigadier Smith (Bill Wallis).

A bomb hits the trench, disrupting a game of I Spy and giving George an excuse to malinger in hospital. Blackadder is sent to hospital, too: a British spy has reported that there's a German spy there somewhere, so the captain has to winkle him out. Darling, however, distrusts Blackadder and goes to the hospital undercover to spy on him in turn. Blackadder suspects the patient who keeps lapsing into German and asking George about troop movements, but he decides to take three weeks away from the trenches to consider it. He interviews suspects, starting with Darling. Meanwhile, Nurse Mary Fletcher-Brown turns out not to be the drip she appears to be, and casual sex ensues. During pillow talk, though, Blackadder realises that she is the spy, and she is hauled off to face a firing squad. Darling, meanwhile, accuses the German-speaking man, only to find that he is Brigadier Sir Bernard Proudfoot-Smith, a British spy who picked up a teensy bit of an accent during his work. It looks as if Blackadder will get to head up Operation Winkle – until he realises that George has been writing letters to his Uncle Herman in Munich all this time.

Watch Out For: Bill Wallis, last seen in 'Head', notches up his third *Blackadder* role.

Cunning Plans: George suggests finding the spy by checking the hospital's list of patients for names that begin with 'Von'. Baldrick's cunning plan is to ask everyone in the hospital if they're a German spy. If it was him, he'd own up.

Cutting Comments: Blackadder, who lost closer friends than George when he was last deloused, refers to the lieutenant's relatives as a 'collection of inbred mutants'. He sums up Darling's new security precautions thus: 'So . . . everyone who comes into the room has to have his bottom fondled by this drooling pervert?' going on to suggest that Darling isn't just doing his job, it's his hobby, too. Baldrick fears that doctors may find him interesting and poke around inside him, to which Blackadder retorts: 'I find the Great Northern and Metropolitan sewage system interesting, but that doesn't mean I want to put on some rubber gloves and pull things out of it with tweezers.' He points out that, if Baldrick's waiting for Miss Right to gather him up in her arms, she'll have to get them out of her straitjacket first, and he accuses his batman of having 'the intellectual capacity of a boiled potato'.

You Horrid Little Man: Blackadder punches Baldrick for failing to understand the complex rules of I Spy. He gleefully takes the opportunity to tie up Darling, put a potty on his head and interrogate him until he's reduced to tears.

Double Entendres: Blackadder doesn't care if Nurse Mary can sing 'I May Be A Tiny Chimney Sweep But I've Got An Enormous Brush'. Operation Winkle has, of course, been set up to winkle out spies (as opposed to spying out winkles, we assume). If Blackadder gets any information then Darling will pump him thoroughly in the debriefing room. If not, Darling will make it very hard for him. George hears that Blackadder has been seeing a lot of Nurse Mary. 'Yes,' the captain confirms, 'almost all of her in fact.' When Mary reveals that her last boyfriend 'bought it', Blackadder assumes she's expecting payment.

Tortuous Similes: George thinks that Blackadder is 'as clever as a chap with three heads.' Blackadder finds Nurse Mary 'as wet as a fish's wet bits' and fears that the spy may be 'as difficult to find as a piece of hay in a massive stack full of needles.'

Blackadder: He visits George in hospital, but only to get hold of the hamper that he knows his family will have sent in. He only smokes cigarettes after making love (he claims to be a twenty-a-day man back home, but later revelations suggest that this is a lie). He loves nurses because they're 'disgustingly clinical'. When asked if he has someone special in his life whom he wants to 'love and cherish and . . . keep safe from all the horror and the hurt', he names himself. He has no girlfriend, having 'always been a soldier, married to the army – the book of King's Regulations is my mistress, possibly with a Harrods lingerie catalogue discreetly tucked between its pages.' There are no casual girlfriends either: when he joined up, Britain was still fighting colonial wars. 'If you saw someone in a skirt you shot him and nicked his country.'

Baldrick: For breakfast, he has tea followed by a little sausage followed by an egg with soldiers. He takes flowers to George, but they've had their heads shot off. He hates 'hosti-pals', ever since his grandfather came out of one dead (although admittedly he went into it dead, too, having been run over by a traction engine). He doesn't want doctors poking around inside him. He's waiting for Miss Right to come along.

George: He thinks Nurse Mary is an absolute peach and reverts to childhood when she mothers him. He denies that his family is inbred, although there is an uncle in Walton-on-the-Naze who's 'seven feet tall with no chin and an Adam's apple that makes him look as if he's constantly trying to swallow a ballcock.' He corresponds with another uncle throughout his stay in hospital, though Nurse Mary has to help him with the German words . . .

Melchett: In his opinion, German spies are 'filthy Hun weasels, fighting their dirty, underhand war' but British spies are naturally 'splendid fellows, brave heroes risking life and limb for Blighty.' His suggested method of extracting a confession is to 'get hold of a cocker spaniel, tie the suspect to a chair with a potty on his head, pop his todger between two floury baps and shout: "Dinner time, Fido!"' He provides Darling with a realistic wound to help him go undercover – by shooting him in the foot. Proof that the Germans know too much comes when they send him a letter saying, 'Isn't it about time you changed your shirt, Walrus Face?' He thinks Oxford University is a dump.

Darling: He is hurt that Melchett never told him about the vacancy for Head of Operation Winkle. Blackadder's insolence makes his blood boil. He smokes. He was born in Croydon and educated at Ipplethorpe Primary School. He has a girlfriend called Doris and he knows all the words to 'God

Save the King', or at least to three verses of it. He breaks down under questioning and cries.

Name Checks: George's Uncle Herman lives in Munich and apparently has Hun sympathies. Field Marshal Haig has a tortoise called Alan.

The War According to Captain Blackadder: He's surprised that anyone could be leaking battle plans, as he didn't know there were any – just a grand scheme to get everyone slaughtered except Field Marshal Haig, Lady Haig and their pet tortoise.

Essential Knowledge: You should never pooh-pooh a pooh-pooh. Melchett once knew a major who made that fatal error: it turned out that the soldier who pooh-poohed him had been pooh-poohing other officers who'd also pooh-poohed their pooh-poohs. In the end, an entire regiment was destroyed by pooh-pooh.

PLAN F: GOODBYEEE

First Broadcast: 2 November 1989.

Field Marshal Haig (Geoffrey Palmer)

There's something in the air, and for once it's nothing to do with Baldrick. The order comes for Blackadder and his men to go over the top tomorrow morning. There's nothing else for it: he has to stick two pencils up his nostrils, put a pair of underpants on his head, say 'wibble' a lot and pretend to be mad. But Melchett's seen that trick before, and had its perpetrators shot, so a rethink is called for. Blackadder still has one chance: over twenty years ago, he saved Field Marshal Douglas Haig's life. It's time to call in the favour. As Blackadder, George and Baldrick reminisce about their time in the trenches, Melchett arranges for a dismayed Darling to be reassigned to the front line. Morning comes, and Blackadder makes his call. But Haig's advice is to stick two pencils up

his nostrils, put underpants on his head and pretend to be mad
. . . With all their cunning plans exhausted, Blackadder,
Baldrick, George and Darling stand ready to charge to their
deaths. Only one phrase befits this situation, and it rhymes
with 'clucking bell'.

Watch Out For: Veteran comedy actor Geoffrey Palmer is
the first *Blackadder* actor since Frank Finlay ('Witchsmeller
Pursuivant') to be given full guest-starring credit in the
opening titles (though there are no closing titles . . .).

Cunning Plans: Blackadder listens to Baldrick's final cunning plan for old-time's sake: it's the one about phoning
Haig, which at least has some merit. Another cunning plan is
mooted just before they go over the top, but what's the point?

Cutting Comments: Blackadder would rather French kiss a
skunk than listen to Baldrick's poems. When Baldrick recalls
that a girl kissed him as he left home to join the army, he
describes her as the 'first casualty of the war'.

You Horrid Little Man: The threat of a bayonet through the
neck dissuades Baldrick from further attempts at poetry.
Blackadder subjects Darling to Baldrick's coffee, but draws
the line at letting his batman sprinkle brown stuff on top. He
sticks a rod up the bottom of Baldrick's dead hamster and
uses it as a dish mop.

Double Entendres: Darling predicts that the Germans will
get a good licking.

Tortuous Similes: George is 'as bored as a pacifist's pistol'.
Blackadder states that the front line has 'moved no further than
an asthmatic ant with heavy shopping'. He faces 'a twelve-
storey crisis with a magnificent entrance hall, carpeted
throughout, twenty-four hour porterage and an enormous sign
on the roof saying "This is a Large Crisis".' George, taken in
by Blackadder's pencils, thinks he's 'mad as a bicycle' – while
he himself is 'as excited as an excited person who's got a special reason to be excited.' We never hear Baldrick's last ever
plan, but it's 'as cunning as a fox who's just been appointed
Professor of Cunning at Oxford University.'

Blackadder: He learned the pencils-up-the-nose trick in the Sudan. In 1892, he was the hero of Mboto Gorge where, according to Darling, the British army 'massacred the peace-loving pygmies of the Upper Volta and stole all their fruit.' On the contrary, though, he and the rest of the 19/45th East Africa Rifles fought 'two thousand Watutsi warriors armed to the teeth with kiwi fruit and guava halves,' and Blackadder saved the future Field Marshal Haig's life from a woman with a sharpened mango. He liked being a soldier, back when the army only fought unarmed natives; for fifteen years, his military experience amounted to 'perfecting the art of ordering a pink gin and saying "Do you do it doggy-doggy?" in Swahili.' Then 'four and a half million heavily armed Germans hove into view.' He played in the football match between English and German troops at Christmas 1914, and still can't believe he was called offside.

Baldrick: He eats cigarettes and makes coffee out of mud, having run out of real coffee thirteen months ago. There's no sugar either: he's been using dandruff since New Year's Eve 1915, and saliva for milk. His mum told him never to trust men with beards, so he doesn't like King George. The idea of French kissing a skunk appeals to him. He writes a poem about war being a horrid thing ('ding a ling a ling'). He and his pals from Turnip Street Workhouse thought that joining the local regiment would be fun. With people cheering and throwing flowers, it was the first time he'd ever felt popular. He loved training, as all he had to do was charge at sacks of straw with a bayonet. 'I remember telling my mum, "These sacks will be easy to outwit in a battle situation."' However, the war has since claimed all his friends.

George: He joined up on 10 August 1914, shortly after he and his fellow Cambridge tiddlywinkers – the Trinity Tiddlers – scored a great victory against their Oxford counterparts. The team leapfrogged down to the recruiting office and played tiddlywinks in the queue. The other tiddlywinkers are dead now, which would be depressing if not for the exciting prospect of going over the top. George arrived at the trench just before Christmas 1914 and, like Blackadder and

Baldrick, played football against the Germans. Faced with the realisation that he's the 'last of the tiddlywinking leapfroggers from the golden summer of 1914,' he realises at last that he's not too keen on dying.

Melchett: He served in the Sudan, too – and shot an entire platoon for putting pencils up their nostrils and pretending to be mad. In 1896, his (rugby?) team thrashed the Old Harrovians 15–4. He claims to have a dicky heart and a wooden bladder. He sleeps with a hairnet over his moustache and expects a promotion to Field Marshal.

Darling: Melchett has come to think of him as a son, albeit an illegitimate, spotty squit that he doesn't like. He hoped he'd get through the war, return to work at Pratt and Sons, keep wicket for the Croydon Gentlemen and marry Doris (see 'General Hospital'). His final note in his diary reads 'Bugger'.

Name Checks: The Trinity Tiddlers comprised Jocko, the Badger, Bumfluff, Sticky, the Gubber, Drippy, Strangely-Brown, Titch and Mr Floppy. A certain pie-shop owner is immortalised in the song 'Whoops, Mrs Miggins, You're Sitting On My Artichokes'. Baldrick's friends, all lost to the war, were Sammy the spider, Katie the worm, Bertie the bird and Neville the fat hamster.

The War According to Captain Blackadder: He can't see how the push can be worth it, given that millions have already died for no gain. George believes that the war started because of the Hun's villainous empire building, until Blackadder points out that 'the British Empire covers a quarter of the globe while the German Empire consists of a small sausage factory in Tanganyika.' He reminisces fondly about the days when the British army never fought anyone with guns – or spears, if they could help it. 'The kind of people we liked to fight most were two feet tall and armed with dry grass.' His plan to feign madness was doomed from the start. 'I mean, who would have noticed another madman round here?'

Essential Knowledge: The war didn't start, as Baldrick believes, when 'some chap called Archie Duke shot an ostrich because he was hungry.' In fact, it started when the Arch-Duke of Austro-Hungary got shot. In Blackadder's opinion, it was simply too much effort *not* to have a war. 'The idea was to have two vast opposing armies, each acting as the other's deterrent . . . [but] there was one tiny flaw in the plan . . . It was bollocks!' So, the poor old ostrich died for nothing.

6: THE
BLACKADDER
LEGACY

Bastard Offspring

Blackadder is still regarded as one of the finest television comedy series ever, so it's a bit surprising that it hasn't been ripped off hundreds of times by TV companies desperate to produce comedy that people actually laugh at. Perhaps, unique as *Blackadder* almost was, they just couldn't find a less than obvious way of imitating it – and they can't have relished the thought of inviting comparisons.

There have been a few more 'historical' comedies – *The Last Salute*, *'Allo, 'Allo* (which actually had a pilot episode before *Blackadder* but didn't become a full series until 1984), *Oh Doctor Beeching!* etc. – but they've tended to owe more to the likes of *Dad's Army* and *Hi-De-Hi!*, by being set within living memory and trading off nostalgia (see Chapter 1). And, although a few sitcoms have been set in earlier times – Channel 4's *Captain Butler* and the recent *The Dark Ages*, for example – they've tended to take entirely different approaches.

Nevertheless, *Blackadder* has undeniably left a legacy, not just in the continuing careers of some of its creators but in the natures of some of the series that came after it.

Here are our favourite examples:

Chelmsford 123

This Channel 4 historical sitcom comes to our attention by not being set within living memory at all; not by a long way. The fact that it began in 1988, between *Blackadder the Third* and *Blackadder Goes Forth* also suggests that its producers hoped to cash in on the success of the BBC series – and indeed the humour is in some ways similar, particularly as regards the suspiciously modern-day sensibilities of supposedly historical characters (lots of language-based puns). If anything, though, the series' outlook was even more modern than that of *Blackadder*; realism is pretty much abandoned as the characters never quite forget that they're actually appearing in a TV series.

This, along with the programme's setting within the Roman Empire more easily calls to mind one of *Blackadder*'s predecessors, *Up Pompeii!*, which we discussed in Chapter 1. As in *Up Pompeii!* the inhabitants of Chelmsford in the year AD 123 exist far from any people or events of import; indeed, the programme's very title trumpets its backwater setting (OK, so the Emperor pays a visit – but apart from that, the nearest we see to real-life historical figures is a brief appearance by the Roman gods Vulcan, Venus and Jupiter, the latter played by *The Black Adder*'s original King himself, John Savident).

Chelmsford 123 was the first series ever produced by Hat Trick, the company that has since been responsible for most of the successful comedy series of the nineties not made by Tiger Aspect. It was written by Jimmy Mulville and Rory McGrath; at the time, both were best known for their roles in the criminally underrated Channel 4 sketch show *Who Dares Wins*, the fourth and final season of which was broadcast immediately after *Chelmsford 123* concluded its first run in 1988. (McGrath is now best known as that incredibly hairy bloke in the comedy sports quiz *They Think It's All Over*.) They brought one of their three *Who Dares Wins* co-performers – two-time *Blackadder* guest star Philip Pope, now best known for writing the music for just about everything Hat Trick do – back in time with them, to ensure that *Chelmsford 123* was very much seen as a *Who Dares Wins* spin-off. Ironically, one of the two cast members that were left behind was a certain Mr Tony Robinson, but then he was probably busy.

'In AD 123,' says the press release for the first episode, 'Britain was a cold miserable dump populated by beer swilling hooligans.' It's also populated by baby-eating Celts, notably Badvoc (McGrath), leader of the Chelmsford tribe, who spends most of his time in the local alehouse and, we're told, doesn't know whether to conquer the Roman invaders or just con them. Mulville plays Aulus Paulinus, whose role as Roman Governor of Britain is less a promotion than a punishment for insulting the Emperor's girlfriend.

Appearing as Badvoc's disgusting cohorts, Mungo and Blag, were Neil Pearson – later to make a name for himself in *Drop the Dead Donkey* and become a big star of both comedy and drama – and Howard Lew Lewis, who had previously played a couple of peasant-type characters in *The Black Adder*. The Celts also counted Geoffrey McGivern among their number – he's still best known for playing Ford Prefect in the radio version of *The Hitch-Hiker's Guide to the Galaxy*, despite having appeared in just about every TV comedy series going since then. Pope played the fawning Grasientus, Aulus's assistant and brother-in-law.

Chelmsford 123 is almost as underrated as *Who Dares Wins*. Channel 4 killed it off after two seasons (allegedly in favour of a chat show with Jonathan Ross); it never seems to get repeated and it hasn't been released on video. It's a pity, really – any series that features a cameo appearance by the TARDIS in its first episode can't be all that bad, can it?

Maid Marian and her Merry Men

To date, *Maid Marian and her Merry Men* is probably the closest thing we've had to a replacement for *Blackadder* – and a well-timed replacement it was too, as its first episode was broadcast two weeks to the day after 'Goodbyeee'. A (drastic) rewrite of the Robin Hood legend, this BBC series was set in the past but, again, featured characters with modern sensibilities. What's more, it was written by Baldrick himself, Tony Robinson, who also starred as perennial gunge victim the Sheriff of Nottingham. OK, so it was officially a children's programme, but who cares? It was far too good for the little sods.

Maid Marian grew out of Robinson's interest in history, and also his concern that children's telly wasn't providing his young daughter with many strong female role models.

Believing legends such as that of Robin Hood to be products
of their times, he decided to reshape that particular one for
the modern age. So, for a start, out went wimpy, weak,
lovelorn Maid Marian, and in came Marian the rough, tough,
confident leader of the outlaw gang – even if this meant
putting something of a dent in Robin's image.

Other characters are similarly familiar and yet unfamiliar.
Friar Tuck loses his religious trappings to become the dim
but nice and usefully strong Rabies (Howard Lew Lewis
again). Little Ron, in contrast to legendary giant Little John,
is actually quite little – but that's all right, because he's three
foot two inches of crazed fighting machine.

Heading up the villains is Bad King John, played as a kind
of evil version of Brian Blessed's Richard IV (i.e., a raving
nutter who shouts a lot) by Forbes Collins, another sometime
peasant from *The Black Adder* (Collins also appears from
time to time as John's brother, Richard the Lionheart). Tony
Robinson's Sheriff pretty much casts off the shadow of
Baldrick by being, apart from Marian, the only vaguely intelligent character in the series. In fact, he's more like Blackadder than Baldrick, although the fact that he's a luckless
figure of fun doesn't help much (a letter to the *Radio Times* in
1989 pointed out that the part was well cast, as Nottingham's
real-life sheriff at that time was called . . . Tony Robinson).

The role of Alan-a-Dale underwent perhaps the biggest
revision, which is fair enough as he was never supposed to be
one of Robin's gang anyway, just someone they met once: he
was grafted on to the legend by Hollywood, when they
wanted a troubadour character to explain the plot by singing
it. Robinson wanted someone like that, too, but not 'some
prat warbling away on the lute.' So, he made his troubadour
the most conspicuously modern member of the gang. Barrington, the world's first Rastafarian, was originally called
Winston, until actor Danny John-Jules (best known for *Red
Dwarf*, but also an accomplished singer and dancer) asked for
a change, on the sensible grounds that *every* black character
on TV at that time was called Winston.

The music of *Maid Marian* is one of its chief attractions.
It's not just Barrington: any one of the characters is likely to

burst into song at the drop of a hat, whether it's the band celebrating 'P-p-p-p-p-p-p-p-pancake Day' or the Sheriff singing about his collection of amusing things to do (putting hedgehogs down his knickers, sitting in bowls of custard, etc.). Lyrics were provided by Robinson himself and set to music by David Chilton and Nick Russell-Pavier of Essential Music. They were recorded before filming and mimed along to on set.

The first episode tells the story of how the band got together, which is probably how it earned its title, 'How the Band Got Together'. Marian comes to (the as yet unnamed) Worksop Village to sell her tadpole, Edwina, but ends up pouring water over the Sheriff of Nottingham instead. She goes on the run, taking Robin of Kensington – owner of a boutique and maker of underwear to King John – along as a hostage. The pair form an alliance, as Marian outlines her dream of leading an outlaw gang who will have pubs named after them in centuries to come. Lured by the promise that he'll be able to design their costumes, Robin travels to Nottingham with Marian and new-found friend Little Ron to rescue the captured Edwina and, incidentally, Rabies and Barrington, who have also fallen foul of John's evil regime and are being tortured with feathers.

During the final confrontation with King John and the Sheriff, Marian notices that Robin's disguise has slipped. 'Robin,' she hisses. 'Hood!' And thus a legend begins, with the king vowing vengeance against the mysterious 'Robin Hood' for the criminal act of torching his voluminous underwear.

A few similar incidents help to cement the premise of the series: that King John and the Sheriff of Nottingham are hunting down Robin Hood, unaware of the real power behind his outlaw band. Whenever Marian and her men – pledged to fight injustice, keep their uniforms clean and do a good deed every day – ride into action, circumstances conspire to make it seem that the cowardly and foppish Robin deserves the credit. Like Henry Tudor's rewriting of the past in *The Black Adder*, this was a clever way of passing off the discrepancy between the story as we know it and as Tony Robinson presented it.

Eventually, Robin begins to believe his own press, and takes to referring to himself by his accidental *nom de plume*. However, his attempt to form a new gang, without girls, is doomed to failure when it turns out that the rest of Marian's followers don't fancy the idea of endless discos and karaoke nights.

As time went by, Robinson expanded the cast of the show. He introduced Marian's childhood nemesis, Rotten Rose Scargill, and gave more substantial roles to some of the extras who played Worksop's peasants. For Season Two, he also added to 'Ye Baddies' (as the credits have it) by recreating Guy of Gisborne as the nephew of King John. Only tolerated because of his vast wealth, the spoilt and childish Guy forces the Sheriff into the role of surrogate parent. He was played by Ramsay Gilderdale, who had previously appeared with Robinson as 'wet halibut' Ralph in *Blackadder's Christmas Carol*.

According to legend, Much the miller's son was one of the original members of Robin's band. However, in *Maid Marian*'s universe, he had to wait until the 1993 Christmas special for his moment of glory (though that's nothing compared to Will Scarlet, who never got to appear at all). Now the son of a mini-mart manager, and a Cockney barrow boy in his own right, Much brings fancy goods – well, clockwork toads – to Worksop. This creates a stir, as the economy – and, for that matter, the diet – of the village is based almost entirely on mud. A smitten Marian asks Much to join her gang, but the offer is withdrawn when it transpires that he is selling weapons to King John as well.

Of the series' numerous other guest stars, it's probably worth mentioning that Patsy Byrne turned up as Marian's mother in the episode 'Keeping Mum'. Although the character is superficially Nursie-like in some respects, Byrne turns in a very different performance.

Maid Marian and her Merry Men was recorded on location in Exmoor National Park, Somerset, with Cleve Abbey providing the authentic twelfth-century stone interiors of King John's castle. Unfortunately, the building's exterior didn't have the necessary 'imposing, evil castle' look, so electronic paintbox effects had to fill in the gaps. Despite the fact that that particular technology was still in its early days, the result is surprisingly impressive and looks nothing at all like a small child has splashed paint on to the television screen.

The hideout of Robin's – sorry, Marian's – outlaw band was then sited in the privately owned Nettlecombe Wood. Worksop, however, was constructed in nearby Hawkcombe, which is open to the public. Recording of the series often had to be fitted around ramblers, sightseers and – at one point – a group of thirty holidaymakers who were brought on a tour of the set by enterprising locals.

For five years, Marian battled for justice, fretted about what her followers would do next to ruin her reputation as a serious freedom fighter and dropped more modern references than you can shake some mud at (Paul the Pig Juggler and his beautiful wife Debbie McGee, indeed). Then, for reasons of their own, the BBC saw fit to cancel the series that had won them awards left, right and centre. Their official reason was that they needed to free up some cash to make other programmes – which only makes sense when you realise how few programmes they actually make nowadays.

Robinson guided the characters through a subsequent run on stage, although sadly few of the original cast were available to reprise their roles. The series also spawned its own imitator, as Mark Billingham – who played hapless soldier Gary and helped out with the writing chores in the fourth season – went on to co-write and star in the rather similar *Knight School* in 1997. This six-part Granada series was set, not surprisingly, in a school for young knights in thirteenth-century England. Tony Robinson got in on the act here, too, acting as script consultant and also making a guest appearance in one episode.

Later episodes of *Maid Marian and her Merry Men* are hard to come by, but the first six have been released on video and episodes from the first two seasons have been adapted into comic strip form by BBC Books. We can only lament the fact that, when Blackadder and Baldrick did eventually meet the inhabitants of Sherwood Forest, they weren't a bit like Tony Robinson had led us to expect.

Mr Bean

Also following hot on the heels of *Blackadder Goes Forth*
was this, Rowan Atkinson's next major TV project. *Mr Bean*
first materialised as a one-off half-hour special, airing on ITV
on New Year's Day 1990. It is of interest to us not just
because of its star but because its script came from all three
of *Blackadder*'s writers – Richard Curtis, Ben Elton and
Atkinson himself – writing together for the first time.

The programme grew out of an idea that Atkinson and
Curtis had for a sketch about a man who couldn't keep awake
in church. The man evolved first into Mr Smith and then into
Mr Bean, and the church sketch duly appeared in that first
special, along with Bean's risible attempts to cheat in an
exam, a beach scene in which he tries to change into swimming trunks without revealing anything he shouldn't, and an
ongoing battle for road supremacy between Bean – in the
yellow Mini that would become his trademark – and the
driver of a three-wheeled Robin Reliant. The humour of *Mr
Bean* comes from the character's childlike nature and lack of
inhibitions, which lead him to go well over the top when
dealing with the normally minor challenges of life. Rowan
Atkinson's expressive features and talent for mime come to
the fore, as few words are spoken, particularly by Bean himself. We've said a lot about Atkinson's versatility, and his portrayal of Mr Bean shows it yet again. The character could
hardly be more different to the various Blackadders – so
much so that, were it not for the personnel involved, *Mr Bean*
wouldn't rate a mention in a book like this.

Despite the popularity of the show, its producers resisted
the temptation to churn out a full series, and continued to
come up with intermittent half-hour specials instead. *Mr
Bean* was followed up, towards the end of 1990, by *The
Return of Mr Bean*: by now, Robin Driscoll had replaced Ben
Elton as co-writer and Howard Goodall had provided a theme
for the character: a classical piece called 'Ecce Homo' (the
lyrics, 'Ecce homo qui est faba, Vale homo qui est faba,'
translate from the Latin to 'Behold the man who is a bean,

Farewell O man who is a bean'). More specials came and went, and Richard Curtis eventually stepped down from the writing chores, leaving Driscoll and Atkinson to continue. Thanks to the physical nature of the comedy, much of Atkinson's contribution was made during rehearsals, as he tried out variations on each theme to see which would look the most humorous.

The team finally called it a day after fourteen episodes, including one that was never broadcast but instead was released on the video *Unseen Bean* alongside an episode that wasn't unseen at all. We have seen Atkinson's character making mountains of many more molehills, from the shopping expedition that ends with him sharing a toilet cubicle with another customer, through the funfair visit in which a soiled nappy is unleashed upon an unsuspecting public, to the meeting with royalty during which he accidentally nuts a princess. We haven't learned much more about his background, except that he's acquired a long-suffering (and unnamed) girlfriend played by ex-*EastEnders* star Matilda Ziegler. We don't even know his first name – it's even listed on his passport as Mr.

We did find out what his job was, though, when Curtis returned to the fold as co-writer and executive producer of the 1997 feature film *Bean – The Ultimate Disaster Movie*, directed by Mel Smith. The film finds Bean working for the Royal National Gallery of London: he sits in a corner and looks at paintings all day. Of course, this being a big-budget movie and all, it's not long before he gets to go jetting off to America, where he causes chaos, most notably by inadvertently defacing *Whistler's Mother* (the script book of the film reveals that this sequence was based on a very early 'Mr Smith' sketch, in which the *Mona Lisa* was the unlucky work of art).

The format of the film differs slightly to that of the TV specials, partly because test audiences got fed up with the extended farcical situations that were the backbone of *Mr Bean* on the small screen. Many of these scenes, then, were cut short – or cut out – in favour of creating a pacier, more focused storyline (some of the missing material appears on

the film's video release, including an impressive and expensive sequence in which Mr Bean – in his Mini – circumvents
road congestion by driving through London's most famous
department store, Harrods). Also, supporting characters were
allowed free rein to use their voices in a way they had never
been used before, although Bean himself remains untalkative.
Well, mostly: a deliberately teasing plot thread leads up to the
moment when the so-called Doctor Bean, having been mistaken for an art expert, has to deliver a speech to the world's
media . . .

Bean – The Ultimate Disaster Movie was a commercial
success, if not an unalloyed critical one. It added another
feather to Richard Curtis's screenwriting cap and became one
of the few British films to ever crack the difficult American
market. It cemented *Mr Bean*'s popularity which, by now,
had grown to eclipse that of a certain other Mr B. Granted,
Blackadder probably has the edge on *Mr Bean* as far as we in
the UK are concerned, but that's more than made up for by
the latter's support overseas. Just try getting on a British-run
plane now without being treated to at least one helping of
Bean's exploits. The show's humour, it seems, travels well,
partly because Bean's taciturn nature cuts down on the need
for subtitles or dubbing. Body language needs no translation.

The Thin Blue Line

It seems that the BBC did want to invite comparisons to
Blackadder when they announced their new situation comedy
about the police force in 1995. Their press release for *The
Thin Blue Line* mentions the then-six-years-gone *Blackadder
Goes Forth* in its first sentence, in the context of it being the
last time that Ben Elton and Rowan Atkinson worked
together for the corporation on a series in which Atkinson
starred and wore a uniform. So, very much the same sort of
thing then.

In this case, the uniform is that of Inspector Raymond
Fowler, the man in charge of the uniformed officers at a small
police station in the fictional town of Gasforth. Traces of
Blackadder do creep into Atkinson's performance – the

original model shows whenever Fowler is flustered, while others pop up as he is required to deliver cutting remarks – but, generally, Fowler is a quite different character. Speaking to *Radio Times*, Ben Elton described him as 'an old-fashioned stick-in-the-mud in a modern situation', which is, of course, the complete opposite of Blackadder. Fowler's abiding morality also sets him apart from Atkinson's earlier creation – although both are, in their own ways, quite conservative – but it is his habitual uncertainty that makes for the most striking difference. Despite his lofty principles, Fowler never quite knows what to do. Indeed, much of the 'sit' in this sitcom comes from his grappling with moral dilemmas or trying to deal with a situation that embarrasses him.

Despite having a central character in the person of Fowler, *The Thin Blue Line* is really an ensemble piece. Elton describes it as 'a sitcom full of completely flawed and bumbling but basically decent people'. He cites *Dad's Army* as an influence, as usual, and it's a much more visible influence here than ever before, as a pompous character is placed in charge of a full complement of idiots in uniform, each competing to prove that their part of the thin blue line is slightly thicker than the rest (that joke comes courtesy of the press release and the first season, both of which use it twice).

As often as not, it is James Dreyfus's portrayal of wimpish, immature, chocolate-loving PC Kevin Goody that steals the show. Goody is dangerously close to being a camp stereotype straight out of a seventies sitcom. But the main difference between him and, say, John Inman's Mr Humphries in *Are You Being Served?* is that Ben Elton made a point of not equating campness with homosexuality. Despite the assumptions of some characters, the viewer knows that Goody can't be gay because we're privy to his unrequited lust for young, forthright, left-wing and well-out-of-his-league WPC Maggie Habib. As the most conspicuously modern character in the series, Habib's primary role is to take an opposing political view to Fowler's.

Sharing Gasforth Police Station with the uniformed officers are the local CID, led by Detective Inspector Grim. Blessed with an over-inflated sense of his own importance and a disdain for modern policing methods and 'political correctness', Grim often comes into conflict with Fowler. Old-fashioned though Fowler may be, Grim doesn't aspire to come much closer to the modern day; where Fowler's attitudes call to mind the 1960s *Dixon of Dock Green*, Grim models himself on coppers from such action-heavy seventies TV shows as *The Sweeney*. He even has a sidekick – although both DC Kray in the first season and DC Boyle in the second are more 'laddish' characters, prepared to humour their boss so long as they can still use their warrant cards to their own advantage.

Rounding out the cast are long-serving and laid-back PC Frank Gladstone and Sergeant Patricia Dawkins, who also happens to be Fowler's live-in lover. Dawkins brings another comedy strand to the episodes, with her continual frustration at Fowler's lack of understanding of the opposite sex. She also suffers occasional fits of jealousy, particularly when it comes to Gasforth's Mayoress, an old flame of Fowler's who finds several excuses to visit the station during Season Two.

The series' humour is more gentle, affectionate and old-fashioned than viewers had come to expect from Ben Elton, his caustic streak almost absent for once. In fact, you could say that this, too, is more in the vein of *Dad's Army* and shows like it, though perhaps it's also a consequence of Elton's writing for *nice* characters for once. As a result, many of his fans didn't take to *The Thin Blue Line*, which is a shame. In our opinion, it's an excellent 'traditional' sitcom, which only receives flak because people didn't expect it to be traditional at all. Now, if Elton had written it under a pseudonym . . .

One thing that is typical of Elton's work is that politics rears its head, albeit in a very thoughtful and even-handed way. This is especially true of the second season, which, perhaps as a reaction to criticism, is a little less gentle, a little more hard-hitting than the first. DI Grim and DC Boyle plant evidence on a man whose guilt they are sure of but can't prove; WPC Habib tries to cover for her sister during a drug raid only to end up on a charge herself; a complaint is laid against PC Goody when, in an uncharacteristic display of anger, he punches a racist thug. These situations are dealt with on a personal level, often providing the sort of moral dilemma over which Fowler loves to dither. In addition, though, *The Thin Blue Line* gives over large chunks of many episodes to the characters' discussions of issues of the day, such as juvenile crime, the arming of the police or the rift between Sir Paul Condon and London's black community (although Goody's contribution to the latter is to point out that the Police Commissioner's surname sounds a bit like 'condom').

Indeed – as in *Dad's Army* – the characters spend more time debating the issues that come with their job than actually doing it. Despite Fowler's insistences that his officers are at 'the sharp end of policing' and poised to deal with the same social problems as any modern-day nick, the emergencies faced at Gasforth tend more towards the 'cat-in-a-tree' type. The town's idea of a crime wave is Student Rag Week, and the greatest affront to society ever encountered by DI Grim is when some lunatic 'dings' his car.

In 1996, Ben Elton told *Radio Times* that *The Thin Blue Line* was 'the thing I have the most special love for. I've always said my favourite shows have been sitcoms and light entertainment shows.' He confessed to being hurt by some of the abuse heaped upon the series by critics. However, it did enjoy a broader appeal. Regularly winning audiences of twelve million, it was voted Best Television Newcomer at the 1996 British Comedy Awards. Sadly, even this wasn't enough to earn it the longer run that – in our opinion, at least – it well deserved.

Let Them Eat Cake

With very nearly a decade having passed since Blackadder went forth for the final time, the Beeb – and Tiger Aspect (them again) – must have thought it safe to put out a programme that was fairly similar. They hedged their bets by casting popular comedienne duo Dawn French and Jennifer Saunders in the leading roles and using that as a selling point. But even so, they were very, very wrong.

A historical setting, powdered wigs and the presence of royalty (the action took place in the Palace of Versailles, the court of King Louis XVI, in 1782, seven years before the French Revolution) ensured that critics could hardly mention *Let Them Eat Cake* without mentioning *Blackadder* as well. And the comparisons weren't favourable – which was a little unfair, as the newer series wasn't *that* bad in its own right, even if the jokes about 'the old Cont' did sometimes wear on a bit.

Let Them Eat Cake was hyped as a 'totally made-up story', which is presumably a rib-tickling reference to the large amounts of make-up consumed by the production. It was created and written by Peter Learmouth, the man behind *Surgical Spirit*, who told *Radio Times*: 'I started looking into the period and it just got dafter and dafter. No wonder there was a revolution. It was a comedy that you could not write: all these people with nothing better to do than chase each other around.'

Jennifer Saunders plays Colombine, the Contesse de Vache (which translates, hilariously, as the Countess of Cow), reputedly the most hated woman in the Palace of Versailles. According to Learmouth, the character was modelled on J Edgar Hoover, 'the idea that this person, by collecting sexual information on other people, had power over them'. He insists that Colombine's penchant for seriously high wigs and her less than pristine hygiene are both realistic traits of the French aristocracy of the time.

Saunders agreed to play Colombine on condition that her long-time partner-in-comedy Dawn French could be her servant. Thus, French and Saunders appeared together in a sitcom not of their own making for the first time, as French took on the role of the insolent, down-to-earth, working-class maid Lisette. Already, it's difficult to avoid comparing the Colombine/Lisette partnership to that of Blackadder and Baldrick, so we won't. The pair best resemble the Prince Edmund and Baldrick of *The Black Adder*, given that Lisette is the one with the brains who must forever bail her mistress out of situations of her own making.

Cast in, dare we say, the Percy/George role of 'another

idiot who hangs around the main character a lot' was Adrian Scarborough as the courtier Bouffant, a gay man of rather dubious morals. Also present at Court, and appearing in several episodes, is Madame de Plonge, social climber and Colombine's chief rival, and her daughter Eveline who, despite claiming that she wouldn't know a penis if she sat on one, is suspiciously well informed in all matters sexual. Like *Blackadder*, *Let Them Eat Cake* isn't afraid to incorporate real-life historical figures into its fiction, even royalty – and so Marie Antoinette (described as 'the king's bit of rumpy') is also a semi-regular fixture, with Elizabeth Berrington portraying a queen every bit as loopy and childish as *Blackadder II*'s Elizabeth. One episode also sees special guest star Richard E Grant cast as the Marquis de Sade, who escapes from the Bastille to subject first Colombine and then Lisette to various sexual indignities, some involving fruit.

The series, like later incarnations of *Blackadder*, was made cheaply on just a few sets. However, a small indoor village set allows another comparison with *The Black Adder*, as Colombine is reluctantly forced to venture out amongst the local disease-ridden peasants, for whom she has nothing but disdain.

Ultimately, the Contesse proves to be every bit as much a history-maker as the Blackadder family: she is visiting Marie Antoinette when she hears of a peasant revolt over bread shortages and, rather arrogantly, shouts 'Let them eat cake!' through the window. In real life, of course, this phrase was attributed to Marie Antoinette herself – although it is indeed debatable whether she actually used it – and was one of the factors that led to her eventual execution by guillotine in 1793.

The BBC placed a lot of confidence in *Let Them Eat Cake*. It was extensively trailered, featured on the front cover of *Radio Times* and accorded the honour of an automatic repeat slot on the Wednesday evening after each Thursday broadcast. At the time of writing, it seems that there will also be a second season, despite the less than stupendous reaction to the first. However, in a development that uncannily parallels the early history of *Blackadder*, the show's producers have reportedly been told that they must deliver more jokes to the pound.

Well, just more jokes full stop, really. Which isn't a bad idea at all.

Chelmsford 123

A Hat Trick Production for Channel 4; 1988–1990
13 episodes; 30 minutes.

Aulus Paulinus (Jimmy Mulville)
Badvoc (Rory McGrath)
Grasientus (Philip Pope)
Functio (Robert Austin, Season One)
Mungo (Neil Pearson)
Blag (Howard Lew Lewis)
Wolfbane (Geoffrey McGivern)

Written by Rory McGrath and Jimmy Mulville;
directed by John Stroud (Season One);
Vic Finch (Season Two);
produced by Denise O'Donoghue,
with Adrian Bate (Season Two).

SEASON ONE (1988; 6 EPISODES)

1. Arrivederci Roma (9/3)
2. What's Your Poison? (16/3)
3. The Girl of My Dreams (23/3)
4. One for the Road (30/3)
5. Vidi, Vici, Veni (6/4)
6. Peeled Grapes and Pedicures (13/4)

SEASON TWO (1990; 7 EPISODES)

1. Heads You Lose (9/1)
2. Get Well Soon (16/1)
3. Bird Trouble (23/1)
4. Odi et Amo (30/1)
5. The Secret War (6/2)
6. Mine's a Double (13/2)
7. Something Beginning with 'E' (20/2)

Maid Marian and Her Merry Men

BBC 1; 1989–1994; 26 episodes;
25 minutes except where noted.

Ye Goodies: Marian (Kate Lonergan)
Robin Hood/Robin of Kensington (Wayne Morris)
Barrington (Danny John-Jules)
Rabies (Howard Lew Lewis)
Little Ron (Mike Edmonds)

Ye Baddies: King John (Forbes Collins)
The Sheriff of Nottingham (Tony Robinson)
Gary (Mark Billingham)
Graeme (David Lloyd)
Guy of Gisborne (Ramsay Gilderdale, not Season One)
Rotten Rose Scargill (Siobhan Fogarty, not Season One)

Ye Peasants: Gladys (Hilary Mason)
Snooker (Robin Chandler, not Season One)

Written by Tony Robinson (with assistance from Mark
Billingham and David Lloyd in Season Four);
directed by David Bell; produced by Richard Callanan.

SEASON ONE (1989; 6 EPISODES)

1. How the Band Got Together (16/11)
2. Robert the Incredible Chicken (23/11)
3. A Game Called John (30/11)
4. The Miracle of St Charlene (7/12)
5. The Sharp End of a Cow (14/12)
6. The Whitish Knight (21/12)

SEASON TWO (1990; 6 EPISODES)

1. The Beast of Bolsover (15/11)
2. The Worksop Egg Fairy (22/11)
3. Little Brown Noses (29/11)
4. Rabies in Love (6/12)
5. Rotten Rose part one (13/12)
6. Rotten Rose part two (20/12)

SEASON THREE (1993; 6 EPISODES)

1. The Big Baby (7/1)
2. Driving Ambition (14/1)
3. Keeping Mum (21/1)
4. They Came from Outer Space (28/1)
5. Robin and the Beansprout (4/2)
6. The Great Mud Harvest (11/2)

CHRISTMAS SPECIAL (1993)

Maid Marian and Much the Mini-Mart Manager's Son
(24/12; 45 minutes but repeated as two 25-minute episodes)

SEASON FOUR (1994; 7 EPISODES)

1. Tunnel Vision (5/1)
2. Bouncy Sheriff (12/1)
3. Raining Forks (19/1)
4. The Wise Woman of Worksop (26/1)
5. Robin the Bad (2/2)
6. The Nice Sumatran (9/2)
7. Voyage to the Bottom of the Forest (16/1)

Mr Bean

A Tiger Television/Tiger Aspect production for
Thames/Central; 1990–1995; 13 episodes; 25 minutes.

Mr Bean (Rowan Atkinson)
with recurring guest stars
Matilda Ziegler, Howard Goodall, Roger Sloman,
Nick Hancock, Hugo Mendez, Rupert Bates,
Rupert Vansittart

Written by Rowan Atkinson, Robin Driscoll (2-13),
Richard Curtis (1–7, plus additional material on 10),
Ben Elton (1);
directed by John Howard Davies, John Birkin, Paul Weiland;
produced by John Howard Davies, Sue Vertue,
Peter Bennett-Jones.

SPECIALS

1. Mr Bean (1/1/90)
2. The Return of Mr Bean (5/11/90)
3. The Curse of Mr Bean (1/1/91)
4. Mr Bean Goes to Town (15/10/91)
5. The Trouble With Mr Bean (1/1/92)
6. Mr Bean Rides Again (17/2/92)
7. Merry Christmas Mr Bean (29/12/92)
8. Mr Bean in Room 426 (17/2/93)
9. Do-It-Yourself, Mr Bean (10/1/94)
10. Mind the Baby, Mr Bean (25/4/94)

11. Back to School, Mr Bean (26/10/94)
12. Tee Off, Mr Bean (20/9/95)
13. Goodnight Mr Bean (31/10/95)

Two short sketches and a full-length episode – 'The Bus Stop', 'The Library' and 'Hair by Mr Bean of London' respectively – have been released on video only. Mr Bean has also appeared in several Comic Relief sketches, notably alongside Cilla Black in a *Blind Date* spoof in 1993, and ice-skating with Jayne Torvill ('Torvill and Bean') in 1995. Rowan Atkinson has made several promotional appearances in character, and even played Mr Bean in adverts for M & Ms and the Norwegian grocery chain REMA 1000.

Oh yeah, and there was that major feature film, *Bean – The Ultimate Disaster Movie* (1997).

The Thin Blue Line

A Tiger Aspect production for BBC 1; 1995–1996;
14 episodes; 30 minutes.

Insp Raymond Fowler (Rowan Atkinson)
WPC Maggie Habib (Mina Anwar)
PC Kevin Goody (James Dreyfus)
Sgt Patricia Dawkins (Serena Evans)
DI Derek Grim (David Haig)
PC Frank Gladstone (Rudolph Walker)
DC Kray (Kevin Allen, Season One)
DC Gary Boyle (Mark Addy, Season Two)
Mayoress Dame Christabel Wickham
(Lucy Robinson, Season Two)

Written by Ben Elton; directed by John Birkin;
produced by Ben Elton and Geoffrey Perkins.

SEASON ONE (1995; 7 EPISODES)

1. The Queen's Birthday Present (13/11)
2. Fire and Terror (20/11)
3. Honey Trap (27/11)
4. Rag Week (4/12)
5. Night Shift (11/12)
6. Kids Today (18/12)

CHRISTMAS SPECIAL (1995): Yuletide Spirit (26/12)

SEASON TWO (1996; 7 EPISODES)

1. Court in the Act (14/11)
2. Ism Ism Ism (21/11)
3. Fly on the Wall (28/11)
4. Alternative Culture (5/12)
5. Come On You Blues (12/12)
6. Road Rage (19/12)
7. The Green-Eyed Monster (23/12)

'The Green-Eyed Monster' is sometimes classed as a Christmas Special, as it was broadcast during Christmas week. However, the *Radio Times* believes otherwise, and that's good enough for us. Anyway, the episode isn't at all Christmassy.

Let Them Eat Cake

A Tiger Aspect production for BBC 1; 1999;
6 episodes; 30 minutes.

Colombine, the Contesse de Vache (Jennifer Saunders)
Lisette (Dawn French)
Bouffant (Adrian Scarborough)
Madame de Plonge (Alison Steadman)
Eveline (Lucy Punch)
Marie Antoinette (Elizabeth Berrington)

Created and written by Peter Learmouth;
directed by Christine Gernon;
produced by Christopher Skala.

SEASON ONE (1999; 6 EPISODES)

1. The Pox (9/9)
2. Murder (16/9)
3. The Portrait (23/9)
4. Making Voopee (30/9)
5. A Marriage of Convenience (7/10)
6. The Royal Command Performance (14/10)

7: BLACKADDER
BACK & FORTH

The Next Generation?

As poignant and moving as the conclusion of *Blackadder Goes Forth* was, distraught viewers were able to console themselves by looking forward to the next chapter in the saga. After all, *Blackadder's Christmas Carol* had already given us a glimpse into the distant future and revealed that, despite the usual lack of evidence of any legitimate progeny of Captain Blackadder, his dynasty would continue for quite some time to come.

Naturally, then, speculation was rife as to which post-First World War setting the next member of the family might turn up in. However, most of it proved to be very wide of the mark.

Rumours and Lies (Lies, Mostly)

Even now, it seems that no retrospective article on *Blackadder* is considered complete unless it unearths details of yet another possible series that never was. Some of the rumours were never all that credible to begin with. The next Blackadder, according to one report or another, was to be a hippy (too placid), an astronaut (too heroic), a Tory MP (too much like Rik Mayall in *The New Statesman*), or even a *Dallas*-inspired JR-type figure (well, maybe).

Not surprisingly, the sixties provided a popular choice of backdrop: in one bit of supposition, Edmund was to switch sides and fight the forces of evil as Bat-Adder – presumably with Baldrick the Boy Wonder at his side – in a superhero spoof inspired by the so-bad-it's-bad 60s television series, *Batman*.

From the Beatles in *A Hard Day's Night* to *Spinal Tap*, rock bands have a proven comedy track record (available from all reputable stockists). *The Blackadder Five*, with a background in the pop industry of the sixties, was an idea that Ben Elton and Richard Curtis actually discussed but rejected in virtually the same breath. Had it ever got off the ground, the likelihood is that Rowan Atkinson would have been a Paul McCartney-esque bandleader with Stephen Fry taking a managerial role à la Brian Epstein. Tony Robinson, naturally, would have performed as the band's drummer, Bald Rick.

It's entirely possible that the idea of *The Blackadder Five* sprang from little more than Curtis and Elton wanting to find a title that denoted the fifth series in some unique way – because that's surely where the notion of *Blackadder MI5* came from (and, indeed, a series based in the world of secret agents would have had the advantage of a back-up title in *Blackadder 005*). However, it's likely that everything else concerning this unimaginative piece of idle speculation from early 1998 was invented by someone who'd enjoyed watching Atkinson's other stints with the Secret Service and saw Blackadder potential there.

Atkinson's first foray into the world of celluloid espionage was as incompetent agent Small-Fawcett in the 1983 James Bond feature *Never Say Never Again*, the film that saw the return of Sean Connery to the role he created. He returned to spying for an award-winning series of Barclaycard adverts: as walking disaster area Richard Latham of MI7, Atkinson displayed an even higher level of comic incompetence, which ensured that the adverts were at least as entertaining as the programmes they were spoofing. Incompetence, however, is not really Blackadder's thing, so, even had there been some basis to this rumour, it's difficult to envisage the format working in a Cold War setting. Presumably, for the eponymous spy to maintain the duplicitous nature of his ancestors, he'd have to have been some kind of double agent . . .

Amidst all these theories came a conflicting set of stories, which suggested that the relationships between various members of the *Blackadder* team had become strained during the making of the latter episodes and that this ruled out the possibility of a fifth series altogether. Given that most of the people involved have since worked with each other on various other projects, the alleged behind-the-scenes rifts couldn't have run too deep. However, it was beginning to seem that, faced with the distinct possibility that *Blackadder* was about to turn into a contemporary sitcom, its creators had decided to bring it to a conclusion.

Arguably, this was a timely move. *Blackadder* ended while it was still a cool and funny show, before the obligatory debates about whether it was as good as it used to be kicked in. And what better way for a TV programme to end than with the very scene that would, ultimately, be voted its official zenith?

The public, however, still loved *Blackadder*. They wanted a fifth series, they enjoyed trying to guess its format and the media were more than happy to feed that desire.

Another possible incarnation of our anti-hero caught the public imagination, thanks to the *Daily Mirror*, in January 1998 – and quickly became perhaps the most tenacious of all the rumours thus far. This time, Rowan Atkinson was reportedly to play a retro-Blackadder some centuries before the character's 'original' incarnation. Controversially, the series was to be set at the time of Jesus Christ, with Blackadder (surely an anomalous name for a biblical character) cast as a scheming and manipulative thirteenth disciple. While this particular rumour had a little more plausibility than others, what with the new millennium being so close at hand, official denials swiftly followed.

Again, this topic would have been covering old ground. The New Testament territory was well and truly explored in *Monty Python's Life of Brian*. This was a film with which Atkinson was all too familiar, having appeared in the classic *Not The Nine O'Clock News* sketch 'General Synod's Life of Python', when the Pythons were being assailed with indignant criticism from the religious fraternity.

The rumour mill has been suspended recently, in favour of actual true reports of a *Blackadder* Millennium Special. Already, though, there's more talk of Blackadders to come, perhaps in a feature-length movie. And perhaps, some day, Richard Curtis and Ben Elton will indeed come up with an identity for a modern-day Blackadder that allows him both the potential for evil and the opportunity to wear dark clothes: a traffic warden, say, or a football referee.

In the meantime, though, the absence of new television episodes hasn't left *Blackadder* fans quite as deprived of new products as most people might think.

Blackadder OBE

Millions of viewers are probably unaware that the Blackadder family welcomed a new arrival into the world in 1991; what caught them out was the change of medium. *The Totally Stonking, Surprisingly Educational and Utterly Mindboggling Comic Relief Comic* was a special tie-in publication produced to raised funds for Comic Relief. The issue was published by Fleetway, home of Judge Dredd – but, because of its charitable objectives, lots of characters from other comic book companies were also allowed to appear within its pages. This meant that the futuristic lawman could compete with Desperate Dan, Captain Britain and Dan Dare to find the biggest chin in comics, only to be pipped for the title by Bruce Forsyth.

Brucie was just one of a host of comedians, or at least artistic representations of them, who appeared in the comic. Some, like Comic Relief stalwarts Lenny Henry, Jonathan Ross and Griff Rhys Jones were expected, as were the likes of Dawn French and Ben Elton. Others – Sid James and Frankie Howerd, for example – were more of a surprise, mainly because they were dead (still, in the world of comics, death has never been as conclusive as you might expect).

With a plethora of superheroes and TV personalities to incorporate into it, the narrative leaps about quite a lot – but one major sub-plot features one Edmund Blackadder, the meanest, stingiest bastard in England. This latter-day Blackadder is a mega-rich businessman, complete with moustache and OBE. After he refuses to donate even fifty pence to Comic Relief, he is taken on a journey of discovery by a disabled girl.

But the cold-hearted capitalist is left unmoved by the suffering he witnesses, and even takes the money the young girl has already collected to cover his expenses. Ultimately, he remains the only person in the country not to have made a donation, and the world is thus imperilled (this all ties in with another sub-plot, which involves Griff Rhys Jones being taken over by aliens – but it's all too complicated to explain). However, having promised the disabled girl some money if she can make him laugh, he is dismayed to find himself chuckling over one of her jokes. He sticks to his word and coughs up.

Baldrick, the faithful butler at Blackadder Castle, puts in an appearance only at the very end of the comic, when he's instructed by Mr B to list its contributors. These include many well-known names from the comic industry and, on both the editorial and writing teams, Richard Curtis.

Despite the wealth of talent involved, *The Comic Relief Comic* was destined to be a one-off. In all honesty, this wasn't surprising: although of interest to comic book fans, it was a bit too right-on and not especially funny. In many ways, it was the ideal accompaniment to the always worthy but often disjointed event itself.

Happy Birthday, Your Royal Highness

In November 1998, after an absence of almost a decade, Edmund Blackadder made a brief and pretty much unheralded return to television, albeit on ITV. However, although it got shown on the box, this was really an example of *Blackadder* on stage. ITV were merely televising a gala that had been held at the Lyceum Theatre on 28 October to celebrate the fiftieth birthday of HRH Prince Charles; the short sketch in which the character appeared had served to introduce the event. The gala, as it turned out, was pretty much upstaged by former Spice Girl Geri Halliwell showing herself up with a rendition of 'Happy Birthday', complete with kisses blown towards the guest of honour.

Written by Ben Elton, the untitled *Blackadder* segment is a prequel of sorts to *The Cavalier Years*, inasmuch as it is set in the same historical period and more or less features the same characters. Rowan Atkinson plays Lord Blackadder, the Privy Councillor at the Court of King Charles, who fully expects to become Privy Attendant as soon as Oliver Cromwell takes power. Sadly, Baldrick doesn't appear in the sketch, although he does get a name check in the dialogue. For the second time in *Blackadder* history, Stephen Fry portrays King Charles I. But this time, he draws upon his portrayal of General Melchett for a reinterpretation of the seventeenth-century English monarch. In *The Cavalier Years*, of course, he played Charles very much as a gentle send-up of his modern-day namesake. It is possible that Fry, who played a big part in the organisation of the evening's entertainment, didn't want to risk offending the birthday boy in the audience, even though the Prince is particularly known for his sense of humour. It's more likely, though, that Melchett-style shouting and baah-ing were considered better suited to the threatening tone of the dialogue.

The sketch, which doubles as an introduction to the real event, sort of echoes the scene in the *Blackadder Goes Forth* episode 'Major Star' in which Melchett is after someone to organise a concert party. It begins with Blackadder com-posing a letter in which he declines to organise the King's birthday gala on the grounds that he would rather go to Corn-wall and marry a pig. No sooner has he finished than the King pops in to confirm that he's going to organise the Royal Gala. Charles mentions in passing that Lord Rumsey has voiced certain misgivings about the celebrations. Then he tells Blackadder to go and kick Rumsey's arse and give him a good clout round the head – adding that his arse can be found in a ditch in Tyburn while his head resides on a spike at Traitor's Gate. All of a sudden, Blackadder warms to the idea of arranging the event. Pretending to be as excited as a masochist who's just been arrested by the Spanish Inquisi-tion, he demonstrates his introduction to what he promises will be the most exciting piece of entertainment since Bernard the Bear-Baiter got rid of the big brown cushion and got himself a real bear.

The Whole Damn Dynasty

Fortunately for the dozen or so people who don't have the *Blackadder* videos, publishers Michael Joseph compiled the scripts for all four series – but not the specials – into a single volume entitled *Blackadder The Whole Damn Dynasty 1485–1917*. This was released in hardback in 1998, with a paperback reprint the following year. In actual fact, the scripts contained therein aren't exactly the same as the episodes, although they are very, very similar. For example, you might find a 'funny codpiece' instead of a 'furry one'. Which is to say, they're transcripts rather than actual scripts, if you see what we mean.

The book also features some new material, which is lent extra weight as it is credited to John Lloyd, Richard Curtis and Ben Elton. Alongside such oddities as the menu from Mrs Miggins's coffee house, Baldrick's school report and Captain Darling's application for Emergency Transfer to Somewhere Much Safer are several hitherto-unseen extracts from the Blackadder Chronicles. These expand upon – and occasionally contradict – the revelations contained in the *Radio Times* article that accompanied *Blackadder the Third*, and introduce us to more new Blackadders than we could possibly have hoped for.

The first part of the Chronicles, erm, chronicle the period from the dawn of history to 1484. For reasons discussed in Chapter 4, the validity of these early proto-Blackadders is in doubt. Some may argue that, as mere dramatisations of the Chronicles, the TV episodes may have taken certain liberties with historical facts. Yeah, like we're going to believe that!

Apparently, the earliest recorded family member was the Druid Edmun, an overseer of the building of Stonehenge. One of the construction workers on the site was called Bad Reek; it doesn't take much imagination to speculate how that name might have evolved over the centuries.

Next up for chronicling is one Blaccadda, a man who saw little future in being an Ancient Briton and so embraced the lifestyle of the Roman invaders. He and his descendants particularly enjoyed the orgies and corruption – but then, who wouldn't?

There's not much more to report until William the Conqueror rewarded the Duc De Blackadder with his title for coming up with the idea of a Doomsday Book, thus showing the Normans the best places to steal from. Here, we find a reference to Castle Blackadder where, it seems, there is 'Absolutely nothing to be found'.

At the time of the Crusades came Blackadder the Chickenhearted who, unlike his King, Richard the Lionhearted, didn't necessarily feel that the best way to spread the message of Christianity was wholesale slaughter in the Holy Land.

Cowardice also played its part in the Blackadder family history during the Hundred Years War, or the Hundred Years Hide as they knew it. Spending the duration of the war in a cupboard under the stairs, the whole family emerged when hostilities ceased, but returned with the outbreak of the Wars of the Roses. This brings us rather dubiously to the advent of the televised instalments.

The Chronicles do nothing to shed light upon the direct offspring of Prince Edmund Plantagenet. However, they do find one Cardinal Blackadder – father of the Elizabethan Blackadder as seen on screen – at the Court of Henry VIII during the time of the early Tudors. The cardinal, apparently, was made Keeper of the Privy Rolls, and Baldrick became the King's seventh wife – a marriage understandably left out of many academic works on the subject. Later, the events of *The Cavalier Years* are detailed in a paragraph or two, which also reveal that the Blackadder of this period changed sides again after Cromwell's death. What a surprise! And then there's the unlikely tale of the genuinely heroic Duke of Blackadder. Queen Anne offered to reward this great general with a palace named after a battle site if he emerged victorious. Fortunately, he went on to lose the Battle of Shithole.

The later parts of the Chronicles are mostly concerned with the Victorian Blackadders. Some were Empire builders like Lt Edmund Blackadder VC of the 21st/34th Lancers who wound up at Rorke's Drift and would no doubt have been more than happy to hand it straight back to the Zulus if it meant that much to them. Others – Elegant Eddie Blackadder for instance – looked for fame and fortune closer to home. Eddie became a music hall sensation with patriotic ditties such as 'Let's Shove, Shove, Shove (A Bayonet Up A Frenchman)'. Then there was the engineer, inventor and evolutionary theorist Isambard Kingdom Blackadder, who became responsible for Darwin's *Origin of Species* when he surmised that Baldrick's brain must be remarkably similar to a mollusc.

Several other Blackadders of the age attempted to gain favour by making unsubstantiated boasts. Physicist E E Blackadder claimed to have made little holes in the sides of biros (oh really? We thought that was Edmund T Blackadder during the Second World War. Just goes to show that you can't believe everything you read). Also, a Doctor Blackadder reckoned that he'd already developed penicillin when Fleming announced his discovery, but had chucked it away because he hadn't liked the name much.

A Doctor Blackadder was present at Queen Victoria's side during her last moments, in 1901, though the Chronicles don't reveal whether it was the same one or whether, indeed, another doctor altogether might have been able to do something. In fact, the Chronicles don't attempt to say anything amusing about this Blackadder at all, although they do go on to compare the next few English monarchs with Captain Haddock out of *Tin-Tin*, which is pretty funny.

But what's this? No entry for Ebenezer Blackadder whatsoever! Surely some kind of oversight and not a deliberate omission – or could this be evidence that Ebenezer returned to his kindly, generous ways and as a consequence was stricken from the family annals? Nah, shouldn't think so. Perhaps they just didn't want us to remember that, in *Blackadder's Christmas Carol*, Ebenezer is said to be the sole survivor of the Blackadder line.

The revelations continue. In 1909, Captain Blackadder of the Antarctic said he'd reached the South Pole before both those other explorers. His achievement had gone unnoticed by them as he chose to wear a light-coloured summer suit, what with it being July and all.

The Chronicles then conclude with a look at Captain Blackadder's pre-First World War career, in which, shockingly, the details relating to the incident at Mboto Gorge differ from the version of events described in the *Radio Times* article that accompanied *Blackadder Goes Forth* (the pygmies are armed with entirely different kinds of fruit).

Rounding off the contents of *The Whole Damn Dynasty* is a brief history of Comic Relief (to which the writers' royalties were donated) – so brief in fact that it neglects to mention *Blackadder – The Cavalier Years*. However, the book's most interesting and unexpected revelation is held in reserve for the back-cover blurb, in which astonished readers are informed that the despicable Baldrick was Blackadder's catamite! Hmm, not the kind of relationship we'd been led to assume at all. It's a wonder there was any Blackadder dynasty at all, if that's what went on between episodes.

Bits and Pieces

Comic Relief's Red Nose Days always provide an opportunity to see various *Blackadder* actors doing their bit for charity. Sadly, though, *The Cavalier Years* remains unique as the events' only real contribution to the canon. Nevertheless, Tony Robinson has been known to don his Baldrick garb now and then to make appearances (usually unscripted) for this and other worthy causes. Most notably, it was as Baldrick – in a costume similar to that of the character's Regency incarnation – that he acted as compere (or 'compost', as Baldrick had it) to Comic Relief's Debt Wish Show. Held at the Brixton Academy in June 1999, this concert was designed to promote awareness of – and ultimately bring an end to – Third World Debt, a cause close to Richard Curtis's heart. 'My friend Mr Blackadder says it's gonna be as funny as a large turnip being inserted into my backside,' said Baldrick of the forthcoming entertainment. 'So, I hope he's right.'

Rowan Atkinson performed in the Debt Wish Show, too,

but sadly not as Mr B. In fact, nowadays, you're more likely
to see him in character as Mr Bean than as Mr Blackadder. If
you want to see him coming perilously close to the latter,
though, then check out his performance in the *It's a Royal
Knockout* special of some years ago.

Perhaps Prince Edward's a *Blackadder* fan – he even calls
himself the Earl of Wessex now, which is surely some kind of
homage – and that's why he asked Rowan Atkinson to get
involved in this much-unloved spin on the *It's a Knockout*
formula. You could say that this was a case of life imitating
art – you know, like the royal influence over various Blackadders. Oh all right then, forget it. Anyway, Atkinson portrayed the extremely Adder-esque Lord Knock of Alton (the
show was made at Alton Towers, you see).

Perhaps the reviewers were disappointed not to see the
Queen Mother and Prince Philip don giant foam heads and go
one-on-one atop a slippery pole or something, but the show
got a critical mauling. It could have been worse, though:
Keith Chegwin could have been in it.

Atkinson played another Blackadder-like role during
Comic Relief 1999. Fans were delighted to hear that he was
due to appear as the ninth incarnation of a well-loved character who hadn't had his own BBC series since 1989 – but it
just happened to be *Doctor Who* fans who were celebrating.

Written by Steven Moffatt (*Press Gang*, *Joking Apart*,
Chalk), 'Doctor Who and the Curse of Fatal Death' was a
four-part combination of a typical *Doctor Who* adventure and
jokes. It also incorporated some of the more outrageous
tabloid stories about the classic science-fiction show that had
seen print over the years (the Doctor getting off with his companion, regenerating into Joanna Lumley, etc.). According to
Richard Curtis, playing the Ninth Doctor enabled Rowan
Atkinson to fulfil a longstanding ambition – but anyone
tuning in partway through could have been forgiven for
thinking they were watching a new *Blackadder* sketch. Clad
in dark raiment, apparently from a bygone era, the Doctor as
depicted here is as cunningly devious as his enemy, the evil
Master (Jonathan Pryce).

As it turned out there were to be more similarities between

Doctor Who and *Blackadder*, with 'The Curse of Fatal Death' all but constituting a trial run for the time-travelling exploits that would provide the premise for the next outing of a genuine, honest-to-badness Blackadder.

Time for Blackadder

At around the time that various spokespersons were denying reports of a biblical series, strong hints were being dropped that there would be a *Blackadder* for the millennium. In fact, it transpired that it was to be a *Blackadder* for the Millennium Dome.

When the New Millennium Experience Company decided to commission a comedy film for screening in the Dome's adjacent cinema – then known as the Baby Dome – *Blackadder*, given its association with so many eras of the old millennium, was the natural first choice. There were backup plans to do an *Only Fools and Horses* special if the *Blackadder* team weren't interested; fortunately, if there was one thing guaranteed to entice them into reuniting it was the chance to make an episode for the big screen. That and the opportunity to be representatives of Britain's cultural heritage for the last thousand years. OK, if there were two things guaranteed to get the team back together . . .

This proved to be a smart move for the Dome people, generating a lot of much-needed positive publicity for their controversial project. *The Blackadder Millennium Film*, as it was first dubbed, was officially launched at the Montreux Television Festival in April 1999, a NMEC spokesman saying '[*Blackadder*] is the best of British comedy to show to the world. Our sense of humour and our comedy is one [sic] of our greatest exports.' Tony Robinson was on hand to help plug the film, saying, 'This is very flattering – it's going to be like the great Crystal Palace Exhibition in the last century, and the Festival of Britain, so it's great to be involved.'

After going by the name *Time for Blackadder* for a while, the half-hour film eventually became *Blackadder Back & Forth*. The usual team of Richard Curtis and Ben Elton provided the script, although in less time than they'd have liked.

Elton admitted in a radio interview that he did it because it was a case of 'Your country needs you'. He was slightly dismissive of the Millennium Dome project as a whole, however, saying: 'I think we're the only thing they've got for the Dome, frankly – and all for £57 per family.' Curtis, who wrote in the midst of campaigning for the end of Third World debt, summed up the movie thus: 'It's all an irreverent trek through British history – a time travel adventure story consisting entirely of people who are either rude or stupid.'

Back . . .

The film, a joint venture between Sky Television, Tiger Aspect and the New Millennium Experience Company – with the BBC getting a nod due to Head of Comedy Geoffrey Perkins' input – was filmed during May and June 1999. Studio work was undertaken at Shepperton Studios, and several outside locations were utilised; for example, Hankley Common in Elstead, Surrey stood in for the area surrounding Hadrian's Wall.

The majority of *Blackadder*'s extended family returned to the fold, with most being given the opportunity to extend their characters' dynasties into new eras. Star billing, however, is given to Rowan Atkinson and Tony Robinson, who recreate Blackadder and Baldrick both in the modern day and in Roman times. Today's Blackadder is a dapper, beard-sporting Lord of the Realm, who comes across as being more self-interested than actually cruel. It's difficult – but not impossible – to imagine that he's a newly enobled version of the character who appeared in the *Comic Relief Comic*. His clean-shaven ancestor appears only fleetingly, but is cast in the 'long-suffering victim' mould of his First World War era descendant.

A rare quote from Atkinson appeared in an early press release: 'Bringing Blackadder to the big screen has always been an ambition. I am delighted to be realising it to celebrate the arrival of the 21st Century. But I'm a bit worried at the prospect of travelling through time with Baldrick.' Of his other persona, Robinson revealed, 'A lot of people say they see Baldrick as an everyman character and, if that's true, then I don't think it says much for the British character.'

Copious publicity material for the film revealed the current identities of Blackadder's other cronies, including details that didn't make it on to the screen. Hugh Laurie's character – simply 'George' in the film – is more formally known as Lieutenant the Viscount George Bufton-Tufton. The descendants of Melchett and Darling, however, have forgone the military life and followed the example of an earlier Melchett by opting for the church instead. Stephen Fry is the surprisingly mellow Bishop Flavious Melchett, with Tim McInnerny as Archdeacon Darling. By reprising the role of Melchett's subordinate in several time zones, McInnerny consolidates the obsequious Darling's status as part of the *Blackadder* company, and by doing so drives the final nail into Percy Percy's coffin. A French Duc de Darling has echoes of another McInnerny character in that his accent is identical to the one put on by the Scarlet Pimpernel while disguised as Frou Frou.

Movies like *Elizabeth* and *Shakespeare in Love* had recently shown that there was still an audience for historical drama and comedy, arguably paving the way for *Blackadder*'s return. Presumably their popularity explains why initial press reports claimed that Miranda Richardson would be competing for the role of Elizabeth I with Cate Blanchett and Judi Dench, who had portrayed Elizabeth with great aplomb in the aforementioned films. Ultimately, however, there could be only one Queenie. It may be inaccurate to conjecture that Miranda Richardson's modern-day character, Lady Elizabeth, is a descendant of the so-called Virgin Queen – but is it any less likely than some of the others producing offspring?

The film's recreation of the Elizabethan era also facilitates the welcome return of Patsy Byrne as Nursie. Sadly, though, Bernard's family tree sprouts no new branches.

A host of big-name guest stars were promised for *Blackadder Back & Forth*. Treble-winning Manchester United manager Sir Alex Ferguson was among those initially invited to appear (most likely in the Hadrian's Wall segment).

Although apparently amused by the idea, he politely declined. In fact, the actual number of guest stars in the film turned out to be quite small, although a lot of publicity was given to the casting of Rik Mayall and supermodel Kate Moss as Robin Hood and Maid Marian respectively. Appropriately, Mayall's Robin is very much in the Lord Flashheart vein, right down to his 'Woof' catchphrase (although the fact that he and Marian practically recreate the Flashheart/Bob relationship makes it seem odd that Gabrielle Glaister wasn't cast in the latter role). Moss, a self-confessed fan of the series, jumped at the chance to appear. Perhaps hinting at her character's destiny, she said: 'Blackadder and Baldrick are just so brilliant, but Queenie is my favourite. She's just a brat with loads of power – not that I relate to that in any way!'

A valuable look at the making of *Blackadder Back & Forth* appeared in the *Sunday Times Magazine* in October 1999, when Matthew Gwyther reported on the set at Shepperton, having visited during June. There he encountered Richard Curtis, who is no stranger to film-making. 'You get to the eleventh take of a line on film and realise that, 10 years ago, if we'd been in the studio doing a TV *Blackadder* you'd only even do a second take if the set fell down. TV is a lot less precious.' Commenting on another difference between the media, Miranda Richardson recalled: 'The audiences were quite important to the original series. They'd usually had a warm-up done by Ben [Elton], and by the time we came on they were well warm. They loved the mistakes we made.'

Interestingly, the article covers the development of a piece of dialogue intended for Hugh Laurie that was omitted from the finished version of the film. The line began life as: 'I'm as excited as a person who's just bought a jam doughnut only to discover that he's got a double portion of jam.' Following suggestions from the cast it evolved into: 'Gosh, this is as exciting as discovering that, due to an administrative error, the new boy in dorm is in fact a girl with a large chest, a spirit of adventure and no pants.' It then got ruder and had to be edited, but rather too heavily it seems.

Forth ...

Previews aside, the PG certificate film opened in the renamed Skyscape cinema (it was sponsored by Sky TV, you see) on 1 January 2000. Potentially fifty thousand people per day could see Baldrick's bare arse on the twenty-metre screen if the auditorium filled for each screening (there were plenty of spare seats when we saw it).

The opening titles suggest that the Blackadder family get everywhere, consisting as they do of a number of doctored images that place Rowan Atkinson everywhere from the Bayeux Tapestry to Margaret Thatcher's side. There's even a picture of an oddly dressed 'Blackadder' alongside a Queen Victoria who looks nothing like Miriam Margolyes.

The action begins at Blackadder Hall (well, it's called that in the publicity material) where the unlikely premise that Baldrick has built a working time machine (one of those particularly clever ones that move in space too) unfolds, enabling himself and the current Lord Blackadder to visit various eras of the past and future – though not the building of Stonehenge, the Battle of Hastings or the time of the Black Death as had been reported.

Apparently the issue of broadcast rights caused some friction between the BBC and Sky, with the former feeling that Blackadder was their character and the latter believing – rightly, as it happened – that their financial input gave them a better case for showing the film first. Frankly, though, it doesn't have the feel of a BBC project. Remember when we suggested that *The Black Adder* had an expensive look about it? Well forget it, compared to this it looks cheap. Thanks to the £3m budget, there's an impressive dinosaur, Elizabeth I's court is spacious and has people in it, the Duke of Wellington is in a proper field (instead of standing in front of painted scenery like the last time we saw him) and there's even a *Star Wars*-style outer space dogfight.

The film's blatant product placement also sets it apart: Blackadder brandishing a Tesco Club Card is the last thing you'd expect to see in a BBC production. His attempts to explain the concepts of supermarkets and bonus points don't impress the gift-hungry Queenie, but they do allow the Tesco logo to linger in shot. Incidentally, Tesco sponsored the Millennium Dome's Learning Zone.

Nevertheless, the film makes a positive effort to fit into the *Blackadder* mould that goes beyond its brief return to the characters and setting of *Blackadder II*. As well as playing various Melchetts, Stephen Fry recreates his 'Duel and Duality' role as the Wellington (although he gives a much more laid-back portrayal, bereft of even a single Melchett-style 'Baah!'). And all the expected cunning plans and tortuous similes materialise too, although with much of the action being set in the present day and beyond there's not a lot to be suspiciously modern about. The plight of Roman versions of the characters, assigned to the front line at Hadrian's Wall, also brings to mind the closing moments of 'Goodbyeee'.

Alas, the presence of a Blackadder (or Blaccadda?) in Roman times – and in the time of Robin Hood too, although we don't see him – confirms the suggestion of The Blackadder Chronicles that Prince Edmund, Duke of Edinburgh, was not the originator of the dynasty. So, Donald, Third Duke of Argyll must have been Donald Blackadder after all; in fact, is it too much to speculate that the Roman Blackadder as seen here changed sides rather than being killed by the Scots and thus originated the Scottish branch of the family tree, which eventually... oh, all right then, we give up.

The big question is: does *Blackadder* succumb to the curse of most other popular TV sitcoms which transfer to the big screen and end up nowhere near as good as they were? The answer, sadly, is yes.

'It's a very different Mrs Miggins's fish pie from the original TV series,' said Matthew Gwyther in the *Sunday Times Magazine*. 'This is inevitable, because the medium is different and it's a one-off. But it does not have the pace and headlong urgency of the TV scripts.' However, he singled out Rik Mayall's performance for praise. For the *Independent*, David Lister opined: 'the much-hyped, specially made *Blackadder* . . . proved more laboured than hysterical and had to resort to controversy-courting moments such as casting Kate Moss as the Queen and remarking: "At last a Queen who looks good naked."' (What's controversial about that, then?) In mitigation Ben Elton told Teletext: 'We had to do the whole 2000 years in 28 minutes, it was pure frustration, in that it was all we could do.'

A Bastard on the Throne

Thanks to press reports, it was no surprise for most people when *Blackadder Back & Forth* ended with the title character changing history so that he became the current King of England. Indeed, by a miracle of time travel (but more to do with Richard Curtis's word processor), the *News of the World*'s *Sunday Magazine* even interviewed the royal couple, Edmund and Marian, along with Prime Minister Baldrick in December 1999.

Foremost among Edmund III's priorities is to reinstate the divine right of kings to sleep with anyone they fancy at a party. And, looking ahead to the festive season, His Majesty explains that, as the nation has grown tired of the formality of the Christmas address, he intends to break with royal tradition and deliver his speech from a Caribbean island, whilst on a high diving board with a bikini-clad Gail Porter sitting on his shoulders.

Edmund's missus, Queen Marian, reveals the secret of how she keeps her figure despite all those state banquets: she lets Boris Yeltsin (who presumably remains a world leader in the altered timeline) eat most of her food. Finally, the Prime Minister divulges that he plans to make the monarchy more relevant in the twenty-first century by giving the King total power over everything but the price of a dog licence. A former Republican, Baldrick was converted after 'mature consideration' and being strung up by his three softest parts for ten days, mainly the latter.

With a Blackadder having finally achieved his family's longest-held ambition, it seems that The Blackadder Chronicles have come to an appropriate end. The closing credits of *Blackadder Back & Forth* may promise a sequel in Summer

3000, but the opening titles proclaim the film to be the final instalment. However, there is a glimmer of hope, with the writers at least seeming reluctant to say goodbye to the character for good. In his interview for Teletext, Ben Elton commented: 'If someone said to me "Let's do a music hall one in 1890," I'd be happy. I can't work out why Baldrick and Blackadder are funny, but they are.' He also resurrected one of those old rumours: 'I'm hooked on that '60s period, which would be great, you know, Blackadder and Baldrick as a pop double act.' Meanwhile, Richard Curtis told *DVD Review*: 'We like the idea that when we wrote the first *Blackadder* we were young and scornful, so we love the idea of being old and scornful, of being old men who use the sarcasm of Blackadder to attack what's happened to the world since we were young.' He suggested that the series' next incarnation would be set in modern times. 'One idea we had was that Blackadder should be a very fed up and corrupt university don and Baldrick would have been his "Scout" for the last forty years, so they would in effect have been married for forty years.'

All this reaffirmed Elton's earlier remarks in the *Sunday Times Magazine* feature: '*Blackadder* is not finished,' he stated. 'We'll never give up on it. It could be a middle-aged show. We'll never officially close it down. Ever.'

Blackadder Back & Forth

Written by Richard Curtis and Ben Elton;
directed by Paul Weiland;
produced by Sophie Clarke-Jervoise.

First Opened to the Public: 1 January 2000.

All Blackadders (Rowan Atkinson)
All Baldricks (Tony Robinson)
All Melchetts (Stephen Fry)
All Georges (Hugh Laurie)
All Darlings (Tim McInnerny)
All Elizabeths (Miranda Richardson)
Dinosaur (Tyrannosaurus Rex)
Nursie (Patsy Byrne)
William Shakespeare (Colin Firth)
Robin Hood (Rik Mayall)
Maid Marian (Kate Moss)
Napoleon Bonaparte (Crispin Harris)
Duke of Wellington (Stephen Fry)
Newsreader (Jennie Bond)

31 December 1999: Lord Blackadder intends to play the best
New Year's Eve prank ever. With the aid of Baldrick, a fake
time machine and a hidden props store, he will convince his
friends that he's collected authentic treasures from the past. A
Roman Centurion's helmet, the Duke of Wellington's original
wellington boots and a two-hundred-year-old pair of underpants (Baldrick's own) will each win him ten thousand

pounds. But the time machine works, and Baldrick is forced to throw the fake trophies at a marauding dinosaur before discovering that his undies make a more effective weapon. Unable to navigate, Blackadder and Baldrick visit the court of Elizabeth I, the far future during a space war, Sherwood Forest, the Battle of Waterloo and Roman Britain, encountering familiar faces as the machine seeks out their DNA across time. Finally, Blackadder dunks Baldrick in the toilet until he remembers how the machine's controls were positioned when they left 1999. They arrive home with their genuine spoils, to find they've changed history so that the Battle of Waterloo was lost and Britain is under French rule. Blackadder travels in time again to reverse his mistakes. But, having learned what a difference one man can make, he hatches a very cunning plan indeed.

Watch Out For: Stephen Fry's additional role as Wellington earns him two credits. Colin Firth found fame in serious period dramas, notably *Pride and Prejudice*. The closing song reminds us what Kate Moss is famous for (i.e., looking good naked). Jennie Bond is the BBC's royal correspondent. Tyrannosaurus Rex is probably a pseudonym, as Equity have no dinosaur actors by that name on their books.

Cunning Plans: Wellington has a plan to defeat the French at Waterloo; it's not cunning, but it is superb, brilliant and completely original. Baldrick, of course, has a proper cunning plan: it consists of drowning Blackadder until, at the point of death, his life flashes before him and he can see how all the knobs and levers in the time machine were originally set. With a tiny alteration, the plan works – although Baldrick wishes he'd flushed the toilet first. Blackadder's final and most cunning plan is to alter history in such a way as to procure the British throne for his dynasty at last.

Cutting Comments: Blackadder suggests that people should refer to 'Robin Hood and his bunch of complete lunatics' or 'Robin Hood and his band of merry morons'.

You Horrid Little Man: Lord Blackadder once persuaded Darling to donate a kidney to him as an April Fool's joke.

After getting Shakespeare's autograph, he assaults him on behalf of all the future schoolchildren who will be forced to study and act in his plays, and again on behalf of those who saw Kenneth Branagh's film version of *Hamlet*. Consequently the playwright gives up his profession, but finds fame as the inventor of the ballpoint pen. The time machine kills the Duke of Wellington, but that's an accident so we'll let it go.

Double Entendres: Robin Hood intends to impale Blackadder with his 'magnificent weapon' – and Blackadder knows exactly what he's talking about. Indeed, Robin can even make the idea of 'giving it to the poor' sound rude.

Tortuous Similes: Hadrian's Wall is 'about as frightening as a little rabbit with the word "boo" painted on its nose' (which, to the Roman Baldrick, is frightening indeed). Baldrick is 'as thick as clotted cream that's been left out by some clot until the clots are so clotted up you couldn't unclot them with an electric declotter'. The fox that was Professor of Cunning at Oxford University is now 'working for the UN at the High Commission of International Cunning Planning'.

Blackadders: Lord Blackadder has the sword-and-snake motif embroidered on his breast pocket. In his dining room hangs a portrait of a much-decorated Blackadder in army uniform – the facial hair suggests that it's himself, but it could be any one of them. He considers his own practical jokes hilarious. Robin Hood addresses him by name, so there must have been a Lord Blackadder in his time. Blackadder's masterful handling of Hood impresses Maid Marian greatly. Believing himself to be in the 1960s, he intends to find some 'hippy free love'. In Roman times, a Blackadder rose to the rank of Centurion but found himself under the command of General Melchett and assigned to the front line at Hadrian's Wall. Orders to return to Rome came too late, and this Blackadder was probably hacked to death by Scots. The horror of a French-ruled Britain galvanises Lord Blackadder into acting to save his country. In the altered timeline he becomes King Edmund III, enjoys a 98% approval rating and marries Queen

Marian of Sherwood. He dissolved Parliament two years ago and leads Britain 'magnificently and prosperously' into the new millennium.

Baldricks: In 1999, his job is to clean out the septic tank. In the absence of Blackadder's chef, he prepares dinner by coughing over an avocado, and serves wearing one of those aprons with a picture of a maid's uniform on the front – and nothing else. He built the time machine, following Leonardo Da Vinci's instructions to the letter despite being unable to read. Well, he's done a lot of Airfix models . . . He only has one pair of underpants with which, Blackadder thinks, he wipes out the dinosaurs (although, from where we were sitting, it looked like he'd only wiped out one dinosaur). The time machine works, which makes Baldrick 'the greatest genius who's ever lived'. But he used the reels of a slot machine as the date indicator and meant to write the dates on in felt-tipped pen but never got round to it, which is 'a spectacular return to form'. Will Scarlet is very friendly towards him, but apparently Baldrick usually favours sheep. He likes raspberry flavoured lollipops. He left nursery school at the age of eighteen but returned there by the time he was twenty-five. He needs a stronger mouthwash. As Prime Minister Baldrick he remains unmarried – of course – but enters his fifth term of office at the turn of the millennium, with his shirt tail hanging out.

Melchetts: The modern-day Melchett believes that the world needs love. He creates new words such as 'stonsense' and 'damnedsome'. He's heard some rubbish in his time – usually when he opens his mouth. His Elizabethan ancestor has a 'less than orthodox mouthal odour', such that he usually smells as if he's had a stoat for breakfast. The General Melchett of Roman times wears a frighteningly short skirt and his catchphrase is 'Baah-us!'

Georges: George looks forward to the new millennium, and wishes to celebrate with 'a great big slurpy toast'. His Roman counterpart, Georgius, has all the usual blind patriotism and misguided faith in his leaders.

Darlings: The modern-day Darling once donated a kidney to Blackadder, which had to be thrown away when it turned out that his friend was lying about his life-threatening disease. Darling's ancestors fought on both sides of the Battle of Waterloo, as aides-de-camp to both the Duke of Wellington and Napoleon Bonaparte. The latter, the Duc de Darling, wonders why the French want to invade Britain anyway, given that 'their wine is made from the pee-pee of cows and their women all have big beards' (apparently it's because the British call the French 'weeds and whoopsies and big girl's blouses' – although, as Darling points out, they are). Back in 1999, Darling believes Blackadder's trip through time to have been a 'cheap conjuring trick'. Under French rule, he becomes a ballet dancer.

Elizabeths: The court of Queen Elizabeth I was once relocated to what would become Blackadder's house. Queenie wants to punish Blackadder for being cheeky, but isn't sure whether to laugh at him or chop his head off. Melchett persuades her to go with the latter, but she'll let Blackadder off in return for a present. She thinks Polo mints are so tasty that she gives Blackadder her crown – to the delight of today's Lady Elizabeth, who is ecstatic to find that it fits.

Nursie: She thinks it's a pity that Lord Melchett no longer smells like a turd, but she's very amused by Queenie's threat to crush Blackadder's skull like an egg.

Name Checks: Blackadder's usual cook is absent, having been invited to an orgy at the house of celebrity chef Delia Smith. Without the genius of Leonardo Da Vinci, of course, the time machine would not have been possible. Rodney Tricycle invented the tricycle . . . apparently. Shakespeare doesn't know who Ken Branagh is. 'I'll tell him you said that,' says Blackadder, 'and I think he'll be very hurt.' Will Scarlet is 'a poof in tights' and Friar Tuck 'a fat tub of lard with a ridiculous haircut'. With Rome under attack from all sides, the Emperor's response is to poison his mother and marry his horse.

The World According to (the Modern-Day) Lord Blackadder: 'If history has taught us anything,' he opines, 'it is that the story of Man is one long round of death and torture and burning people as witches just because they've got a wart.' He tells Robin Hood's men that he can't understand why they 'give every single penny to these so-called poor, who just sit on their backsides all day laughing at you . . .' He is scornful of Baldrick's assertion that anyone can change the world, believing that real change comes from 'huge socio-economic things' and that all an individual can do is 'try and make a bit of cash'.

The World According to Centurion Blackadder: As the Romans face 'a horde of ginger maniacs with wild goats nesting in their huge orange beards', Blackadder isn't impressed by Hadrian's idea of keeping the attacking Scots at bay with a three foot high wall.

Essential Information: Baldrick's trip through time teaches him that 'human beings have always been the same: some nice, some nasty; some clever, some stupid; there's always a Blackadder and there's always a Baldrick.'